Contents

Published in 1984 by Rand McNally & Company
First published in 1983 by Pan Books Ltd., London
Designed and produced by Piper Books Ltd., 1983

Library of Congress Catalog Card No. 84-60398
Printed by Graficas Reunidas S.A., Madrid, Spain

First printing 1984

SHIPS AND OTHER SEACRAFT

By Brian Williams

Editor: Jacqui Bailey
Series Design: David Jefferis

RAND McNALLY & COMPANY
Chicago • New York • San Francisco

Braving the Unknown

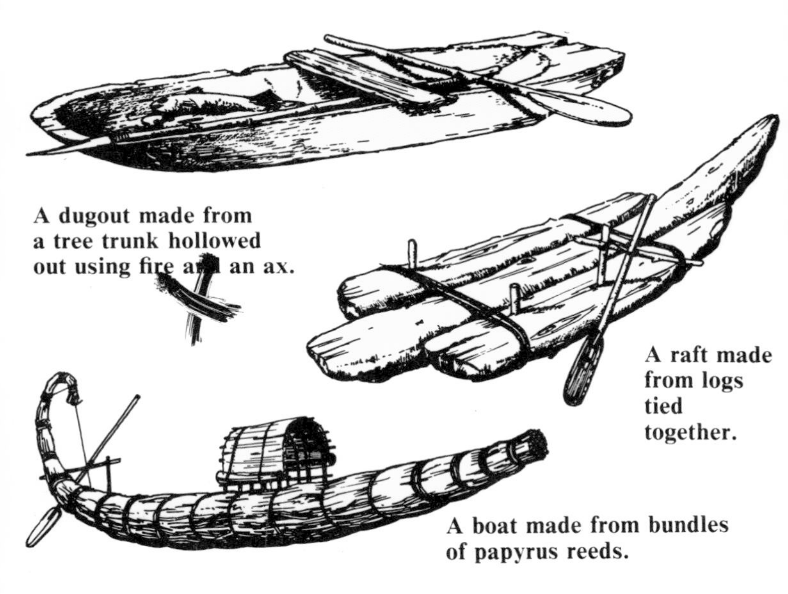

A dugout made from a tree trunk hollowed out using fire and an ax.

A raft made from logs tied together.

A boat made from bundles of papyrus reeds.

We do not know when the first boats were built, but it must have been many thousands of years ago. Today some peoples still use very simple boats. From these we can guess what early boats were like.

Prehistoric people probably saw that fallen trees floated in the water. They then found that they could sit on a tree trunk and paddle with their hands. Rafts were made by tying together tree trunks. Dugout canoes were made by hollowing out tree trunks. And other types of boats were made from animal skins and reeds. The coracle and kayak are two very ancient craft. Both are made by stretching animal skins over a frame. These boats are very light. They can be carried easily by anyone hunting or fishing.

Canoes can capsize, or turn over, very easily. But people soon learned how to stop this from happening. They added an outrigger. An outrigger is shown in the picture opposite. Today's catamaran uses outriggers.

First Voyages

The oldest known pictures of boats are at least 6,000 years old. They show Egyptian boats. There was not much wood in ancient Egypt, so these boats were made of reeds. They were moved with paddles. Such small boats could only have been used on rivers. But the explorer Thor Heyerdahl showed that larger primitive boats could make long ocean voyages. In 1970 he crossed the Atlantic in the *Ra II*. This was a large Egyptian-style reed boat. In 1947 Heyerdahl had crossed the Pacific on the *Kon-Tiki*, a raft made of balsa wood.

Egyptians began to make wooden ships as early as 3000 B.C. They then began to travel on the Red Sea and in the eastern Mediterranean.

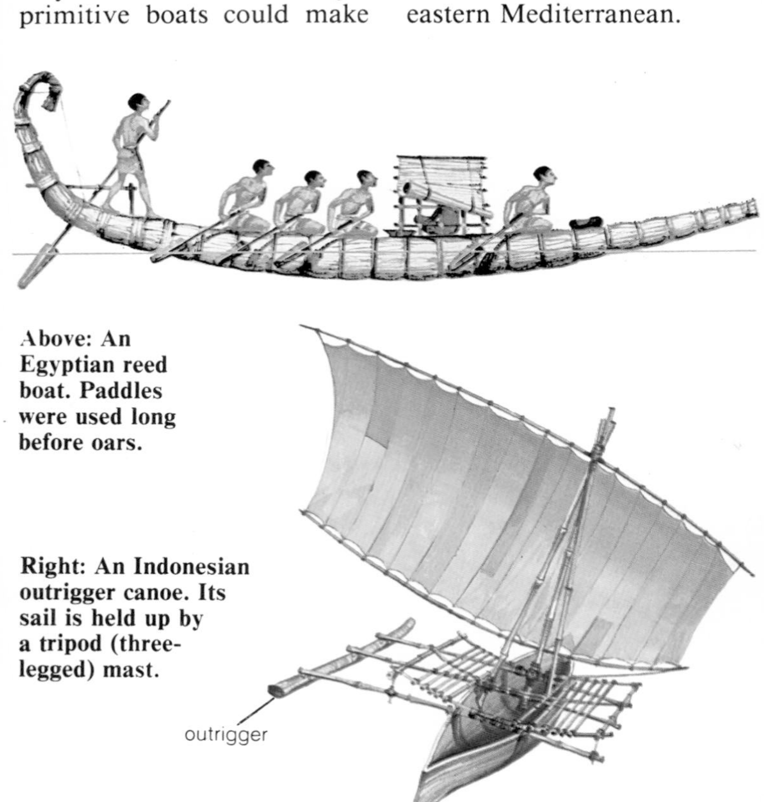

Above: An Egyptian reed boat. Paddles were used long before oars.

Right: An Indonesian outrigger canoe. Its sail is held up by a tripod (three-legged) mast.

Masters of the Mediterranean

The Phoenicians were the best seafarers of the ancient world. About 1000 B.C. they sailed all around the Mediterranean and beyond. Later the ancient Greeks and then the Romans became the masters of the Mediterranean.

All of these seafaring peoples used two basic kinds of ships. One was a warship. The other was a cargo ship.

The favorite warship was the galley. It had many oars as well as sails. The Greek trireme was a galley with three banks of oars. In the largest galleys, 16 rowers pulled each oar. One or two large oars near the stern (back) were used to steer. On the front of the ship was a sharp ram. It was used to break the hull (body) of enemy ships.

The cargo ships of this time were called roundships. The largest Roman roundships were 180 feet (55 m) long and 45 feet (14 m) wide. They looked rather tubby. But they could carry 1,000 tons of grain, oil, and wine across the Mediterranean, from Egypt to Rome. Roundships did not use oars. They were true sailing vessels.

Above: A Greek trireme. It had three banks, or rows, of oars. Smaller galleys (below) had only one or two banks of rowers.

Below: A Roman roundship. It was used to carry goods across the Mediterranean.

Early Voyagers

Right: A Phoenician galley with two banks of oars. It was built of Lebanese cedarwood.

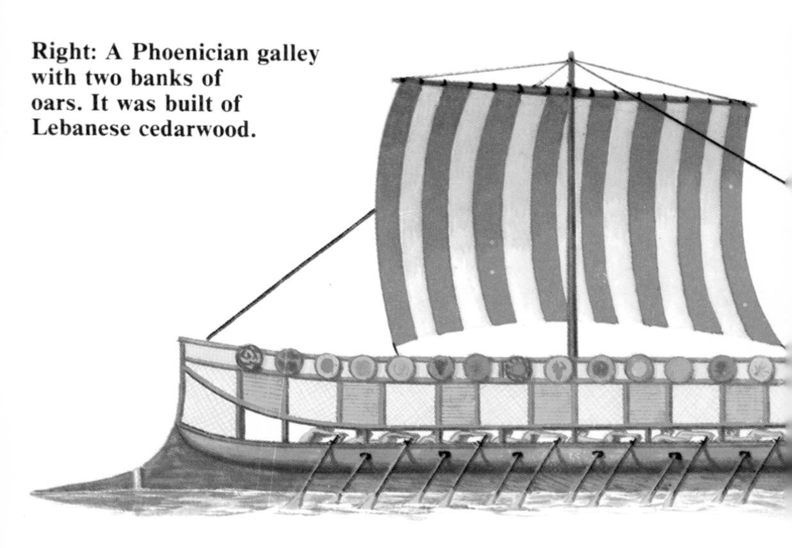

Early sailors did not have maps. They relied on the stars to guide them. Even so, Egyptians, Arabs, and Chinese all sailed far from home. And the Phoenicians sailed all the way from the eastern Mediterranean to Scandinavia.

Viking Raiders

From A.D. 800 to 1050, the fierce Vikings of Scandinavia raided towns all along the coast of Europe and England. They even sailed across the Atlantic to North America.

The Vikings had three main types of ships: the *karv* (a coastal ship), the *knorr* (a seagoing cargo vessel), and the long ship, used for both trading and making raids. The *drakar,* or dragon ship, was the largest of the long ships—160 feet (49 m) or more!

All Viking ships had a single square sail. Large ships had 60 rowers. The steering oar was on the right-hand, or "steerboard," side of the ship. (This is how we get the term *starboard.*) Viking ships were *clinker-built*: the planks overlapped like roof shingles. Mediterranean ships were *carvel-built*: planks were joined edge to edge.

Right: The Vikings sailed from Scandinavia to other parts of Europe. They even crossed the Atlantic to North America.

Below: Viking longships were faster and more seaworthy than any others of the time.

The Great Age of Sail

By the year 1000, the Vikings had declined as a sea power. The other peoples of northern Europe began to trade more and more among themselves. They built bigger and better ships. One of these was the cog. It was sturdy and strong. It was used as a cargo ship and as a warship. The cog had one mast and a single square sail. It also had a rudder. The rudder was used to steer the ship; it replaced the steering

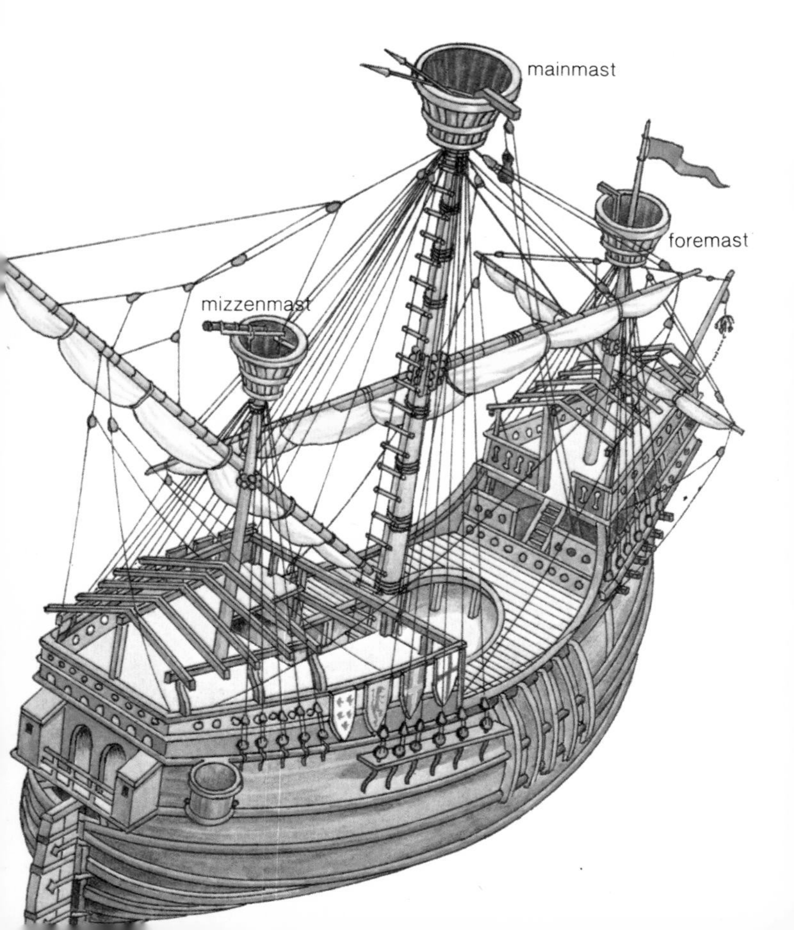

Left: A three-masted carrack. This ship used both square and lateen sails.

Above: No picture of the *Santa María* exists. But she probably looked like this.

oar. These ships also had extra decks, called castles, at the bow and stern. This addition of a forecastle and a sterncastle made the cogs heavy and clumsy.

Change and Adventure

By the 1400s the cog was replaced by the carrack. This ship had three masts. The mainmast was in the center of the ship. The foremast was in the front. And the mizzenmast was at the rear. The carrack carried both square and lateen sails. Lateen sails are triangular. They were copied from Arab ships. These sails made it easier to sail in different kinds of wind. They were rigged on the mizzenmast.

Christopher Columbus set sail for the New World in 1492. His flag ship was the *Santa María.* Columbus did not think much of her. She was too small and too slow, and she was leaky. Columbus did like the *Niña* and *Pinta,* the two other ships that sailed with him. They were caravels. They were smaller than the

Santa María, but they were faster.

The great Portuguese navigators also liked caravels. Bartholomeu Dias was in a caravel when he sailed around the southern tip of Africa. And in 1498 Vasco da Gama sailed to India in a caravel.

Finding the Way

Columbus, Dias, and da Gama were followed by many other explorers. The great European age of discovery came in the late 1400s and early 1500s. European explorers traveled great distances. They went to Africa and Asia. They went to North America and South America. These voyages were made possible by better ship designs. They were also made possible by better navigational aids. The compass had reached Europe from China in the 1100s. It showed navigators which direction was north. The cross-staff, or forestaff, was used to take observations of the sun. This helped the navigator determine the position of his ship. The backstaff was an improved version of the cross-staff. Both are shown below.

Below: The cross-staff and the backstaff. Early navigators used these instruments to measure the angle of the sun above the horizon.

The "Great Ship"

During the 1500s much larger ships were built. One English ship, the *Mary Rose,* could carry more than 400 people. Sad to say, the *Mary Rose*

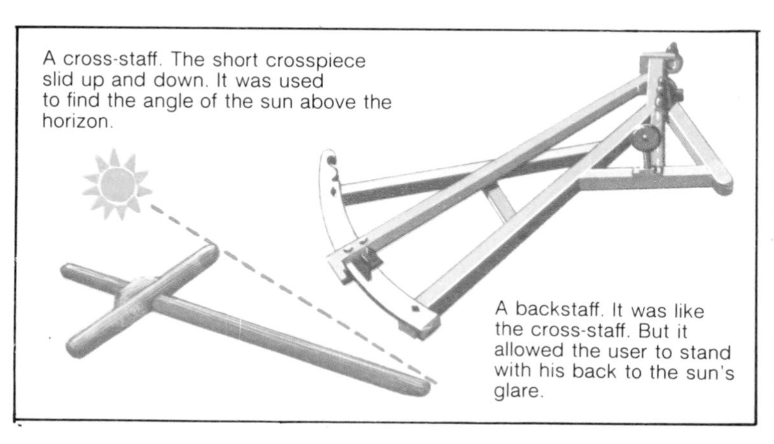
A cross-staff. The short crosspiece slid up and down. It was used to find the angle of the sun above the horizon.

A backstaff. It was like the cross-staff. But it allowed the user to stand with his back to the sun's glare.

sank in 1545. At this time, shipbuilding was a family craft. Shipwrights (people who build ships) did not always use accurate measurements. And sometimes they made mistakes. This happened with the *Mary Rose.*

Still the shipbuilders of the 1500s learned from their mistakes. And they copied good designs of other shipbuilders. What they ended up with was the "great ship"—the galleon. The galleon was used as a warship and as a merchant ship.

Right: A caravel of the 1400s. The Portuguese sailed around Africa in such ships. They used simple navigational instruments to find their way.

Below: An East Indiaman of the late 1700s. These merchant ships were well armed, and could fight off marauding pirates.

The Great Galleon

Ships' figureheads of the 1700s. The figurehead was attached at the bow of the ship. It became the ship's mascot.

The galleon was the most important ship of the 1500s and 1600s. It combined the sleek lines of the galley and the full rig of the sailing ship. Its masts carried two or three sails. The mizzenmast carried one or two lateen sails. Most galleons were fast and sailed well. But some galleon warships were built with high forecastles and sterncastles that made them clumsy.

The English Navy had

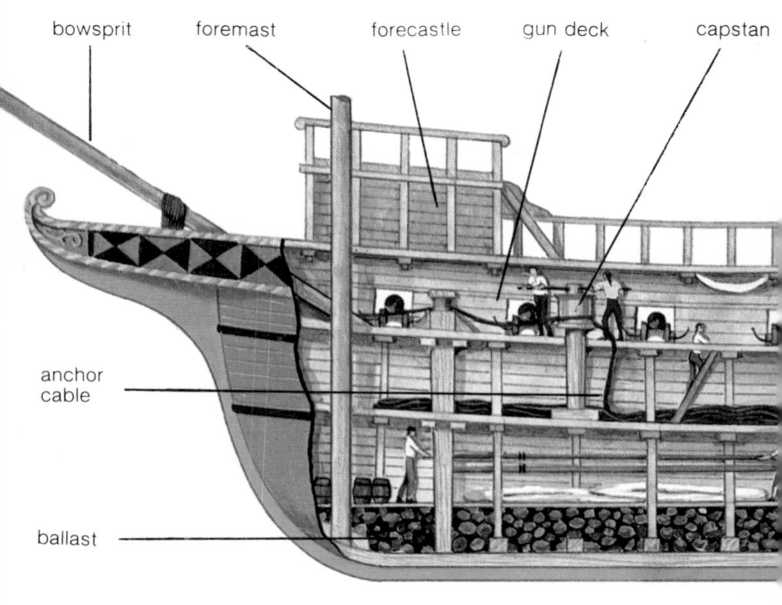

many large galleons armed with big guns. The Spanish Navy also used galleons. But these were very large and slow. In 1588 the Spanish gathered together a huge fleet—the Spanish Armada. The Spanish wanted to conquer England. In a famous naval battle, the English defeated the Spanish.

Galleons were also used as cargo ships. The Spanish used them to bring gold and other treasures back from the New World. But these treasure ships were often captured by pirates in faster ships.

In the 1600s a new type of ship was built to carry cargo. It was called the East Indiaman. (There is a picture of an East Indiaman on page 15.) The first of the East Indiamen were small. But by the end of the 1700s, some were about the same size as the galleons they had replaced.

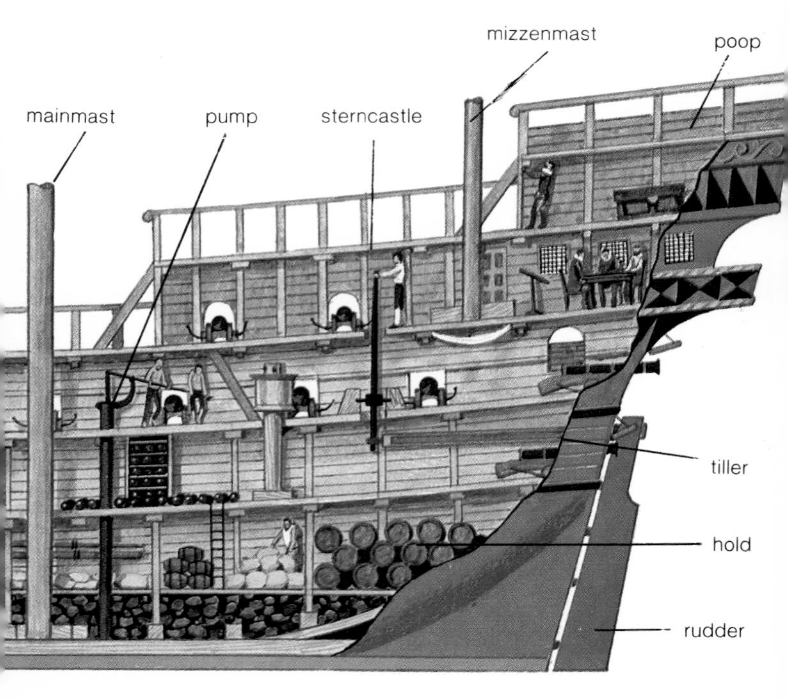

Clippers and Windjammers

Clippers were the most graceful of all the large sailing ships. They were also very fast. In fact, their name comes from the verb *to clip*, which means to move quickly. A clipper could cross the Atlantic in 12 days. One clipper sailed from Japan to California in just 18 days. These streamlined ships carried prospectors to the gold fields of California and Australia. They raced each other from Shanghai to London with cargoes of China tea.

The clippers were first built in the United States, in the 1840s. They were called Yankee Clippers. But soon Canada and England were building them too. Donald McKay, a Canadian, built the *Great Republic.* It was 335 feet long (102 m)—the largest clipper ever built. The *Great Republic* had four masts. Most clipper ships had only three. Some of the larger clippers could set more than 30 sails. The sails and the streamlined hull allowed the clippers to speed along at 20 knots or faster.

A Race Against Steam

With a good wind and a calm sea, a clipper could go faster than a steamer. But a steamer could guarantee its time of arrival. It did not depend on the wind.

Builders of sailing ships made one last effort to compete with the steamers. They built giant sailing ships called windjammers. Windjammers carried huge spreads of sail.

Most had three masts and a steel hull. the *Preussen* was built in 1902. It had five masts. It was the largest sailing ship ever built. From stem to stern it measured 433 feet (132 m). But, by the late 1800s, even these huge sailing ships could no longer compete with the power and reliability of steam.

Above: The windjammer *Preussen.* It had five masts. And it was the biggest sailing ship ever built.

Left: A typical clipper. Most clippers had three masts. Some of the large clippers carried more than 30 sails.

Last of Their Line

Many improvements were made in sailing ships. And every effort was made to keep them in service. But the progress of steamships could not be stopped. By the late 1800s the battle was lost. Steamships were replacing sailing ships on the world's seaways. By 1914 steamships accounted for four-fifths of the world's tonnage.

In the past 100 years many types of sailing ships have disappeared from the seas. Some large sailing ships are still around. But they are used as training ships for naval cadets. Others are museums. The *Constitution*, nicknamed *Old Ironsides*, is at the Boston Naval Yard. The British clipper *Cutty Sark* is at Greenwich, near London. Many interesting sailing ships can be seen at Mystic Seaport in Connecticut.

Today, in the Western world, most sailing ships are used for sport and fun. But elsewhere, sailing craft are still used to carry cargo and passengers. Arab dhows can still be seen. And a few schooners still carry goods in the Mediterranean.

The *Thomas W. Lawson* was built in 1902. It was the only schooner ever built with seven masts.

The Chinese Junk

The junk is another traditional sailing craft that has survived. Junks are used mostly in China and Southeast Asia. They are sailed on rivers and on the seas. Large trading junks are very strong. They can make long ocean voyages. One Chinese junk sailed from Hong Kong to France. This was a 9,000-mile (14,500-km) voyage. Junks have from one to five masts. Most have three. Their sails often look like venetian blinds. They are made of panels of cloth that are spread on bamboo strips.

Right: A traditional English ketch. It was used mostly for coastal work. Ketches carry three or more sails.

Below: The *pechili* junk of northern China. Some junks were 200 feet (60 m) long. Two of the five masts could be removed.

The Triumph of Steam

The first practical steam engine was made in 1712. Early steam engines were used to pump water and run simple machines. In 1769 the Scottish engineer James Watt made an improved steam engine. Many inventors hoped that it could be used to power boats.

A French inventor, the Marquis de Jouffroy, was the first to build a steamboat. In 1783 his ship, the *Pyroscaphe,* traveled upstream on a river for fifteen minutes. Four years later, in the United States, John Fitch built a steamboat. Fitch started passenger service in 1790. But this soon ended. Fitch's steamboat was not very good. In England the same thing happened to William Symington. In 1802 his steamer, the *Charlotte Dundas*, pulled two heavy barges along a canal in Scotland. But his engine was not good enough, and he ran out of money.

Fulton's Clermont

The first successful steamboat was built by Robert Fulton. It was named the *Clermont*. In 1807 it made its first run on the Hudson River. It steamed from New York to Albany. The distance was 150 miles (241 km). The *Clermont* made it in 32 hours. A sailing sloop took four days! The *Clermont* soon began regular steamship service. Fulton also built the first steam warship, the *Demologos.*

In 1809 the *Phoenix* steamed from New York to Philadelphia. This was the first sea voyage by a steamship. The new age had begun.

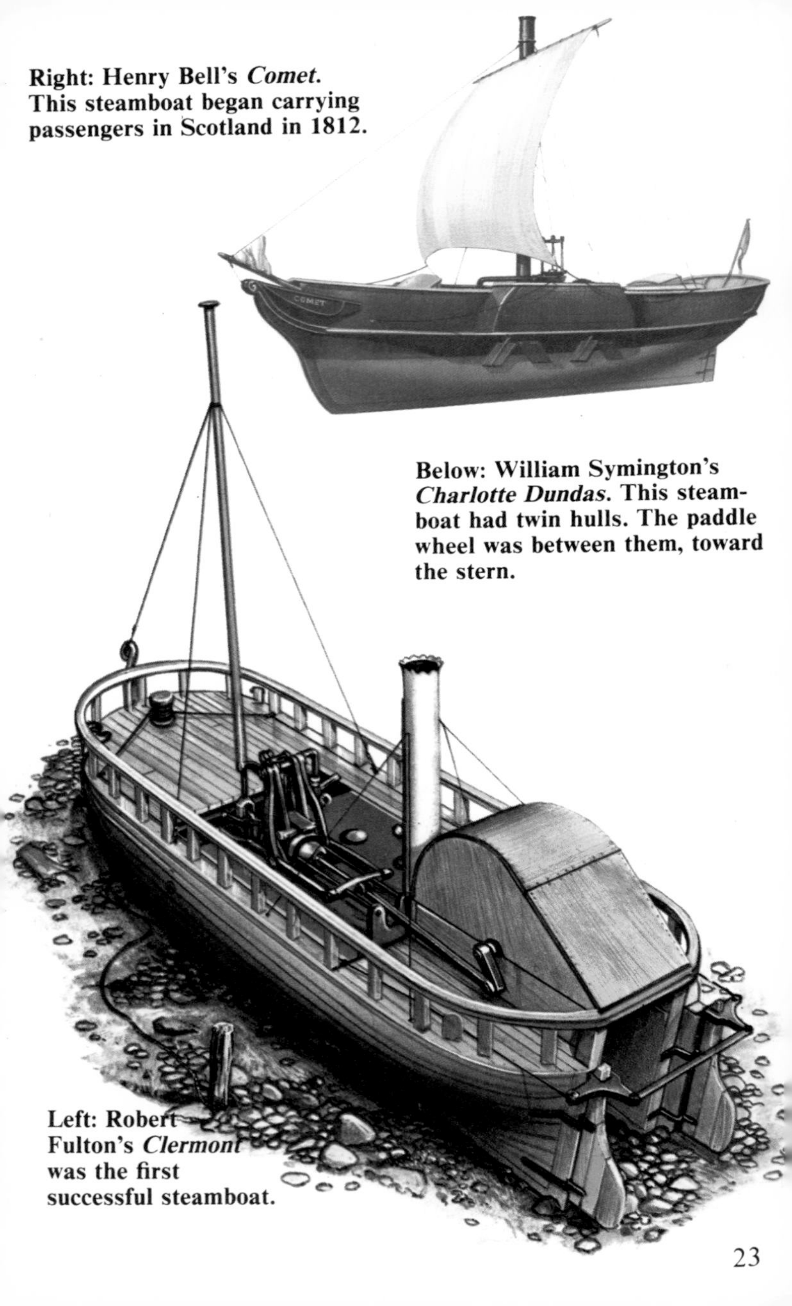

Right: Henry Bell's *Comet*. This steamboat began carrying passengers in Scotland in 1812.

Below: William Symington's *Charlotte Dundas*. This steamboat had twin hulls. The paddle wheel was between them, toward the stern.

Left: Robert Fulton's *Clermont* was the first successful steamboat.

Screws and Paddles

The first steamships were driven forward by paddle wheels. The paddle wheels usually were mounted at the sides of the ship. They were good for river use. But they were not very good at sea. They were often damaged by heavy waves. In a storm the ship would roll, and one paddle would lift out of the water, spinning uselessly.

As early as 1836, inventors made screw propellers to drive ships forward. The propeller was at the stern of the ship. It was completely underwater. A propeller could push a ship forward much faster than a paddle wheel.

A Tug of War

The USS *Princeton* was launched in 1843. It was the first warship to use the screw propeller. Still, some people were not sure that the propeller was better than the paddle wheel. In 1845 a tug-of-war was set up between two ships, the paddle steamer *Alecto* and the screw propeller *Rattler*. People would now see which was better. The two ships

A stern-wheeler riverboat. These ships were the pride of the Mississippi.

In a tug-of-war, the *Rattler* (left) towed the *Alecto* backward.

were linked stern to stern by a cable. Each ship then tried to pull the other. Finally, the *Rattler* pulled the *Alecto* backward. The screw propeller was better than the paddle wheel.

Paddle steamers were still used, however. The first Mississippi River steamboats had been side-wheelers. Now, stern-wheelers replaced them. Stern-wheelers were slower but cheaper to run.

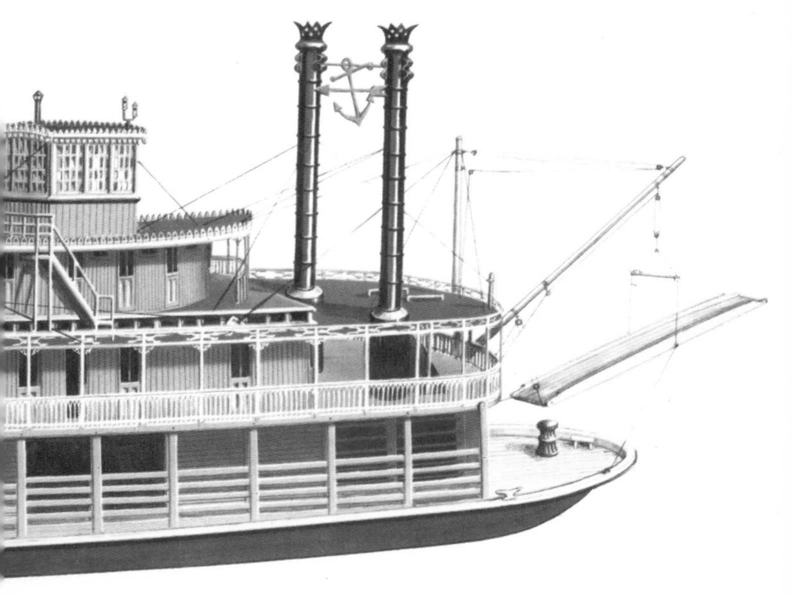

Across the Atlantic

The *Savannah* was the first steam-powered ship to cross the Atlantic. She was a sailing ship, but a steam engine and two paddle wheels had been added. In 1819 the *Savannah* traveled from the United States to England. She took 21 days. but for most of the trip, the sails were used. Still, this voyage pointed the way.

The *Sirius* was the first ship to cross the Atlantic entirely under steam power. She made the trip in 1838. It took less than 19 days. The *Sirius* arrived in New York Harbor just ahead of the *Great Western*. This ship was built especially for Atlantic crossings. It was designed by Isambard K. Brunel, England's most famous ship designer.

Brunel's Dream Ship

Brunel went on to build the *Great Britain* (1843). She was the first large ship to have a screw propeller. She was also the first ship to have an iron hull.

In 1858 Brunel built the *Great Eastern*. No larger ship would be built in the next 40 years. She was also the only ship ever built with screw propellers, paddles, and sails. She was designed to carry

Brunel's *Great Eastern*. This oceangoing ship had sails, paddles, and screw propellers.

Isambard Kingdom Brunel

The *Sirius* was the first ship to steam all the way across the Atlantic Ocean.

4,000 passengers nonstop to Australia. The *Great Eastern* did not perform well. She lost money for her owners, but was used to lay the first transatlantic cable.

Soon steel instead of iron was used to build ships. The first all-steel passenger ship to cross the Atlantic was the *Servia* in 1881.

The New Age

A new age in ship design began in the 1890s. Steel replaced iron and wood. New kinds of engines and fuels were used. Ships became more powerful. They were bigger, and they were faster.

Piston steam engines were used on most ships. These engines were very reliable. But they were very heavy. They were not suitable for high-speed ships.

In 1894 Sir Charles Parsons put a new kind of engine in his yacht *Turbinia.* It was a steam turbine engine. To everyone's amazement, his ship sped along the River Thames at a speed of 34.5 knots (63.9 km/h). Navies began to use turbines for fast warships. Ocean liners such as the British *Mauretania* also began to use them.

Diesel Power

Merchant ships did not need speed. They needed cheap fuel. Most ships at this time used coal to run the steam engines. Coal was expensive, and many men were needed to tend a coal burner.

Rudolf Diesel was a German engineer. In 1897 he made an engine that did not use steam or coal. The diesel engine uses fuel oil. It is cheaper to run than steam turbines.

Diesel engines were first put in ships in 1910. The first ocean-going diesel-powered ship was the *Selandia.* It was launched in 1912.

Above: The Danish *Selandia.* She was the first oceangoing ship to be powered by a diesel engine.

Below: The *Turbinia.* She was the first ship to use a steam turbine.

The Blue Riband

Beginning in the 1870s, ocean liners grew in importance. They brought immigrants to the United States. And they carried travelers to distant countries. Crossing the Atlantic had once been unpleasant and dangerous. Now, for the rich, it was a social event. Some of the new ships were luxurious. And they were fast.

The Quest for Speed

A special thrill for passengers was to be on a ship competing for the Blue Riband (ribbon). This award was given to the liner making the fastest crossing of the Atlantic.

The *City of Paris* (above) and the *City of New York* were the first twin-screw ocean liners.

The *Titanic* struck an iceberg on its maiden voyage. It sank in less than three hours.

The last paddle steamer to hold the Blue Riband was the *Scotia.* This ship was built in 1862. The *Oceanic* and the *City of Paris* also won the Blue Riband. These steamships set new standards of comfort and speed. But they carried sails—just in case. The most famous holder of the Blue Riband was the *Mauretania.* This ship had turbines and could reach a speed of 27.4 knots (50.7 km/h). She held the Blue Riband from 1907 to 1929.

Left: The *Mauretania* was the first ship to cross the Atlantic in less than five days.

Ocean liners like the *Mauretania* were big and powerful. The *Titanic,* for example, had sixteen watertight compartments in her hull. Everyone thought she was unsinkable. The *Titanic* sailed on her maiden voyage in 1912. In the icy waters of the North Atlantic, she hit an iceberg. The *Titanic* sank in less than three hours. More than 1,500 people died.

The *Lusitania* was a sister-ship of the *Mauretania.* In 1915 she was torpedoed and sunk by a German submarine. It was one of the events that led the United States to enter World War I.

The End of an Era

The golden age of the luxury liners lasted for 50 years. To many people they represent an era of elegance. Their size alone amazed most people. The *Titanic* was 46,000 tons. The German Blue Riband holders *Bremen* and *Europa* were 50,000 tons. Yet they were dwarfed by the *Queen Mary* and the *Queen Elizabeth*. The *Queen Elizabeth* was more than 83,000 tons. She was the largest ocean liner ever built.

Apart from size, the great ships had style. They were like beautiful floating hotels. But in the 1950s airplanes were crossing the Atlantic. Passengers could be in Europe in hours instead of days. It meant the end for the ocean liner.

Some liners had met their end during World War II. The *Bremen* was destroyed then. So was the Italian liner *Rex*. And the French liner *Normandie* was destroyed by a fire in 1942.

The *Queen Elizabeth* ended its days as a floating university in Hong Kong. In 1972 she was destroyed by fire. The *Queen Mary* was retired in 1967. She had crossed the Atlantic a thousand times. Today the *Queen Mary* is at Long Beach, California. She is a hotel, museum, and conference center.

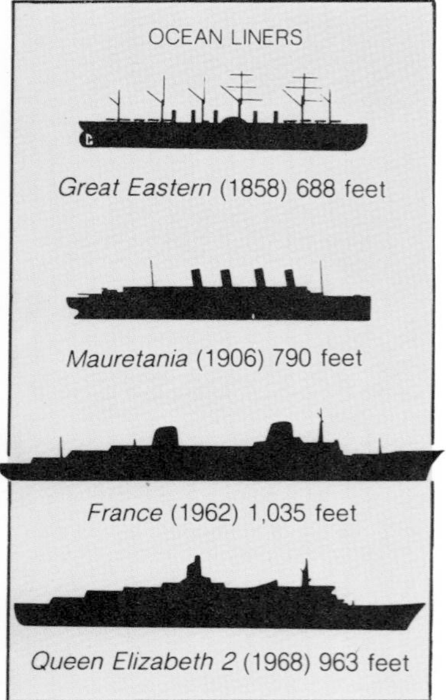

The *France*, now renamed *Norway*, is the longest liner ever built.

The last Blue Riband holder was the *United States.* On her maiden voyage, in 1952, she crossed the Atlantic in three and a half days. It was the first time the U.S. had won the Blue Riband in 100 years. Today the *United States* is in mothballs.

In 1939 there were 86 Atlantic liners in regular service. Today there are none. The *Queen Elizabeth 2,* the *Norway,* and a few others now earn their living as cruise ships. The North Atlantic is left to the jumbo jets.

War at Sea

In the ancient world, war at sea was fought mostly hand to hand. Galleys drove their rams into enemy hulls. Archers, spear-throwers, and slingers hurled their weapons. If a captain was skillful, he could shear off his enemies' oars.

The Roman war galley with "eyes" beneath its prow. Like the Greek war galley, its bow is a battering ram.

Roman galleys carried marines. They would board the enemy ship by means of a ramp. Giant sickles were swung to cut away the enemy's rigging.

The Battle of Salamis was the most important naval battle of ancient times. It was fought in 480 B.C. The Persians had more than 1,000 galleys. They attacked a Greek fleet of about 380

The Spanish Armada was beaten by the faster ships of the English fleet.

ships. The battle took place in a narrow channel. The Persian ships were so crowded together they couldn't maneuver. Then the Greeks attacked, using their battering rams. Many Persian galleys were sunk. The rest fled.

Cannon Fire

Cannons changed the way war was fought at sea. In 1588 they were used in a major naval battle. The Spanish sent an armada to invade England. First the English sent burning ships into the Spanish fleet. Then, when the Spanish tried to get away, the English opened up with their cannons. Their cannons had a longer range than the Spanish cannons. And the English ships were faster, so they could stay out of range of the Spanish guns. As a result, the Spanish fleet was scattered. This battle showed how important speed and firepower are in sea warfare.

A CUTAWAY VIEW OF A LATE-1700s WARSHIP

key to illustration:
(1) upper deck
(2) upper gundeck (gun ports open)
(3) lower gundeck, with the heaviest guns
(4) orlop deck, below waterline
(5) hold, for stores
(6) keel
(7) bowsprit
(8) figurehead

Ships of the Line

During the 1600s and 1700s, warships went into battle in line. These warships were called ships of the line. Beginning in the mid-1700s, fleets were divided into classes. These classes were known as rates. A *First Rate* warship had 100 or more guns. A *Second Rate* ship had 84 or more guns. And a *Third Rate* ship had 70 or more guns.

These warships were supported by still others. A frigate was a fast ship with one gun deck. A sloop had up to 18 guns. Two-masted brigs had as few as six guns. Smaller ships such as bomb ketches, cutters, and schooners were also part of the fleet.

The largest guns were 32-pounders. Sometimes the guns fired solid cannonballs. At other times they fired chain shot. These were balls linked by a chain. Chain shot was used to shoot away masts and rigging. Cannons also fired grapeshot. This was a container packed with small musket balls. It scattered among the enemy. Red hot balls or bombs were used to set enemy ships afire.

On Board

Life was hard for the crew of a warship. It was dark below decks. The air was foul. The food was poor. It is no wonder that navies found it difficult to keep crews. To get sailors, navies would send out press gangs. They would kidnap people and force them to join a ship's crew.

This print from the 1700s shows a press gang. They are seizing men for the Navy.

Warships were quite sturdy. Elm wood was used for the keel. (Elm helps keep out water.) But oak was used for the rest of the ship.

Battleships could serve for years. In 1797 the U.S. *Constitution* was launched. It had 2 decks, 3 masts, and over 50 guns. It was so tough it earned the name "Old Ironsides." It was active until 1880, and is now a floating museum in Boston.

The Battleships

The first iron merchant ship was at sea in 1820. In the 1820s, too, explosive shells were invented. These could blow huge holes in wooden warships. So navies began to think about building iron warships.

The First Ironclads

Some of the first iron warships were actually wooden ships covered with iron plates. The British and French built some of these around 1860. The first duel between ironclad ships took place in the United States, during the Civil War. The Union's *Monitor* fought the South's *Virginia*. The *Monitor* was an ironclad ship. It was the first ship to have a gun turret. The *Virginia* had been converted to an ironclad from the frigate *Merrimack*. The battle ended in a draw, but it meant the beginning of a new type of navy.

The *Virginia* (*Merrimack*) fights it out with the *Monitor* (right).

The *Dreadnought* was the first moden battleship. It was built in 1906.

The British warship *Devastation* was built in 1871. She carried four 12-inch guns. She had no sails, and she was the first warship with a modern look. Beginning in the 1890s the British and others used steel to make warships. These big, heavily armed ships were now called battleships.

The Japanese bought some of these new battleships from Britain. In 1905 they used them to defeat Russia at the Battle of Tsushima. The Japanese ships had long-range guns. They scored hits from as far away as 8 miles (13 km).

The Dreadnought

The first truly modern battleship was the *Dreadnought*. This British ship was built in 1906. She was turbine powered. She could speed along at 21 knots (39 km/h). And she

Yamato

had five gun turrets with ten 12-inch guns. The *Dreadnought* put every other warship out of date. From this time on, battleships were the pride of the world's navies. They would rule the seas for over thirty years.

In the early 1900s other kinds of ships were added to fleets. One of these ships was the battle cruiser. These ships were not heavily armored. But they were very fast. The British ship *Lion*, which was built in 1912, could travel at

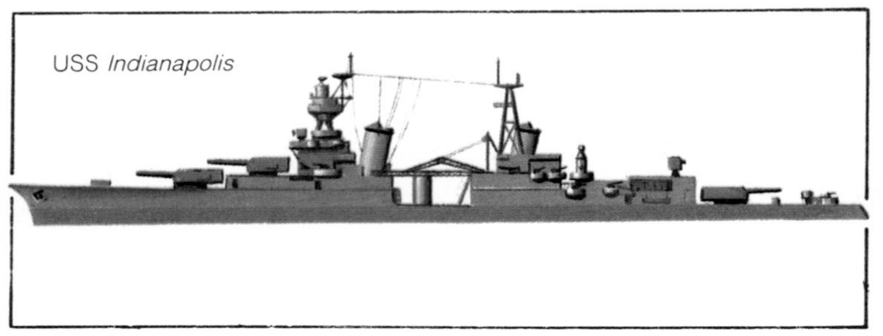

28 knots (51.9 km/h). Cruisers were even smaller than battle cruisers. Both types of ships were used to track and harass an enemy. The battleships would then close in for the kill.

Japan's *Yamato* (top) and her sistership, *Mushashi*, were the largest battleships ever built. They were sunk in World War II. *Indianapolis* (above) was a heavy cruiser.

Battleships at War

The biggest naval battle during World War I (1914–18) was the Battle of Jutland. It was fought in 1916. The British fleet of 151 ships included 28 dreadnought battleships. There were 99 ships in the German fleet. These included 16 dreadnoughts. Neither side really won this battle. Afterward Germany concentrated on using submarine warfare.

The British battleship *Rodney* was built in 1927. It had 16-inch guns.

During World War II (1939–45), airplanes were the most important weapons. And aircraft carriers were the most important ships. Battleships lost their importance. It was too easy for airplanes to sink them.

The Mighty Flattop

The first aircraft carrier was made during World War I. The British took a cruiser, the *Furious,* and added a flight deck to it. The first U.S. aircraft carrier, the *Langley,* was converted from a coal ship in 1922.

Several more carriers were made the same way. In 1927 the battle cruisers *Lexington* and *Saratoga* were rebuilt as carriers. These early carriers looked very odd. They had flat tops (the flight decks) from bow to stern. The British *Eagle* and the U.S. *Ranger* were the first ships to be built from scratch as aircraft carriers. By the beginning of World War II, the United States had four more carriers.

Carriers in World War II

On December 7, 1941 the Japanese attacked Pearl Harbor. The attack was made by planes from aircraft carriers. In the following year American carrier-based airplanes raided Japan.

The Battle for Leyte Gulf was the biggest naval battle in history. It was fought in October 1944. America massed 32 carriers. U.S. forces sank 4 Japanese carriers, 3 battleships, 9 destroyers, and 10

A U.S. *Essex*-class carrier of World War II. It could carry 100 planes.

cruisers, thus destroying the Japanese fleet.

New Types of Carriers

In the 1950s and 1960s, the U.S. Navy built more and larger carriers. One, the *Enterprise,* was nuclear-powered. During the 1970s and early 1980s, several supercarriers were built, such as the *Nimitz*, which is 1,092 feet (333 m) long. It has a crew of more than 5,000. And it can carry about 100 planes. These carriers are very expensive. And they are targets for long-range missiles. Smaller carriers have been designed. They carry helicopters and jump jets. Jump jets can use very short decks.

The USS *Enterprise* was the first nuclear-powered aircraft carrier.

The Modern Navy

Aircraft carriers paid a high price for success in World War II. Forty-two carriers were sunk. Submarines sank 18 of them. And flattops were easy targets for bombers.

Today is the age of missiles. Aircraft carriers and other ships face even greater dangers. For special protection, fleets use early-warning aircraft. They also use ships that are specially equipped to hunt submarines.

The British frigate *Amazon*. Frigates are used for escort and patrol duty.

Frigates and Destroyers

Destroyers and frigates are the workhorses of a navy. Frigates act as the fleet's "eyes." With radar, they watch for enemy ships and planes. They also hunt submarines. Frigates are armed with guns and missiles. Most carry a helicopter. They are lightly armored, but they are fast. They have gas turbine engines. They can travel at a speed of 35 knots (64.8 km/h).

The British destroyer *Sheffield*. It was hit by an Exocet missile.

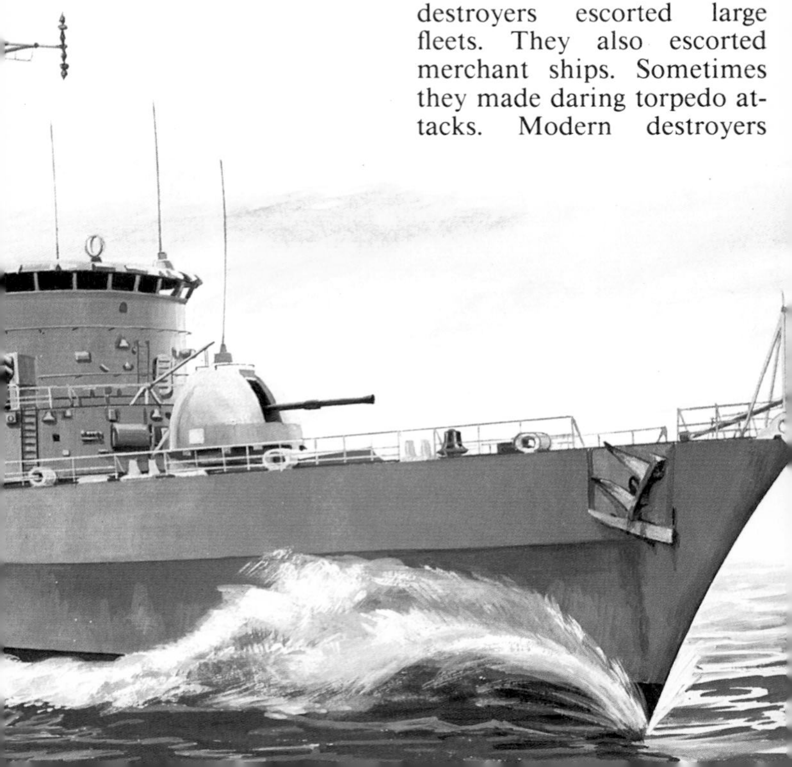

Destroyers are used to protect larger warships. They also bombard enemy positions on shore. During World War I and World War II, destroyers escorted large fleets. They also escorted merchant ships. Sometimes they made daring torpedo attacks. Modern destroyers

have guns and rockets. They do not have armor plating. For this reason, sailors call them tin cans.

The Missile Threat

Modern warships face two major threats. One is the homing torpedo. Submarines carry torpedoes. But torpedoes can also be launched by airplanes and surface ships. The other threat is missiles. Air-launched missiles skim just above the waves. The Exocet missile flies so low that it is hard to spot on radar. How can a ship protect itself from these missiles? It can fire off strips of aluminum "chaff." This confuses the missile's electronic system. The ship can also try to shoot down the missile. Modern warships have rapid-firing guns. They also have antimissile missiles.

Ships at sea also need airplanes to protect them. The planes can be land-based, or they can be launched from aircraft carriers. This protec-

A guided-missile destroyer. Destroyers are heavily armed. They protect larger ships from enemy attack.

tion is especially important when troops are being landed.

The USS *Enterprise* and escorts. This aircraft carrier is the world's longest warship.

Support Ships

In addition to warships, a fleet will have many other kinds of ships. These are called support ships. They include supply ships, tankers, and repair ships. Minesweepers, salvage tugs, and hospital ships are also support ships. (For more about the ships that make up a modern battle group, see page 90.)

Will Big Ships Survive?

Is the big warship out of date? Many people think so. It is difficult to hide a supercarrier like the *Nimitz.* It is easily spotted by airborne radar. Spy satellites can spot it too. Still, ships like this, with their 100 planes, are very powerful. They are a force to be reckoned with.

The U.S. Navy has brought back the battleships from mothballs. The *New Jersey* has seen duty; the *Iowa* became active in 1984. The *Wisconsin* and the *Missouri* will be refitted later. All will carry Cruise Missiles.

Beneath the Waves

In 1776 a submarine was used in battle for the first time. During the Revolutionary War a student named David Bushnell made the *Turtle.* This small, one-person submarine was propelled by a hand crank. The *Turtle* stole beneath the British warship *Eagle.* The plan was to blow up the *Eagle.* The effort failed. But it showed that submarines could be used in war.

Steamship pioneer Robert Fulton built a submarine in 1800. It was named the *Nautilus.* But no navies were very interested in it. They felt underwater combat was not sporting. During the Civil War a Confederate submarine was built. The *Hunley* was an eight-man sub. It attacked the *Housatonic*, a Union gunboat. The *Housatonic* was blown up, but so was the *Hunley.*

The Holland Boats

John Holland was an Irish-American inventor. In 1900 he interested the U.S. Navy in his submarine. They bought it and named it the *Holland.* Holland's submarines were the first true submarines. They had gasoline engines for traveling on the surface. And they had electric

A World War I German U-boat. These ships operated far from land. They sank many merchant vessels.

The *Turtle* was the first submarine to be used in war. It held one person.

motors for use underwater. To make the ship dive, ballast tanks were flooded with seawater. To make the ship surface, the water was blown out of the tanks. This basic system is still used in submarines.

Submarines were used in World War I and World War II. German submarines were called *Unterseeboote,* or U-boats. They hunted in groups known as wolf packs. The wolf packs raided Allied shipping. During World War II they almost stopped American supplies and arms from reaching Great Britain. Altogether they sank more than 3,500 Allied ships.

Miniature submarines were also used during World War II. Japanese miniature submarines took part in the attack on Pearl Harbor.

Right: A British "human torpedo." In World War II midget submarines were used to attack large warships.

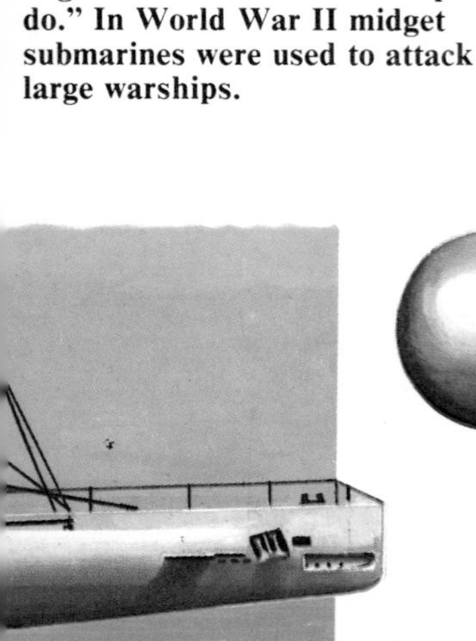

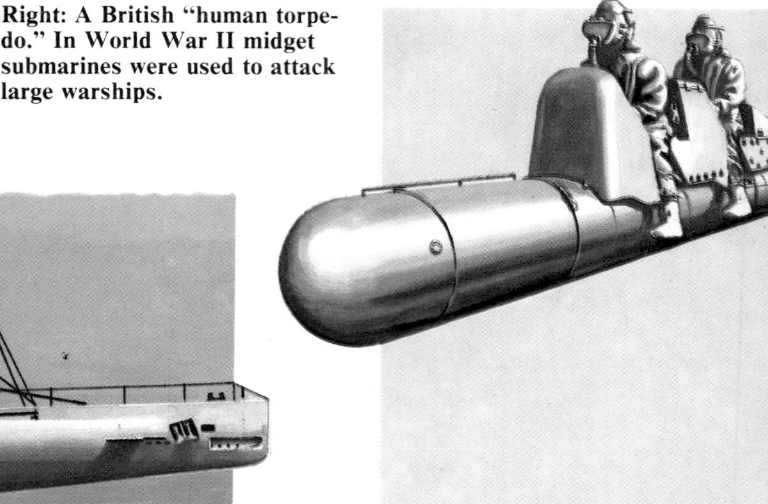

The Modern Submarine

World War II submarines were deadly. They were hard to find. And when they were found, they were hard to destroy. But they also had weaknesses. They had to surface every now and then to recharge their batteries. Also, their diesel engines used up a lot of air. To overcome this, the Germans invented the snorkel. This was an air tube. It allowed the submerged U-boats to suck in air. But this could be done only when the submarine was near the surface. And the snorkel could be spotted by enemy planes or ships.

A missile is launched by a nuclear submarine.

Nuclear Power

Nuclear submarines can stay under water for a long time. The nuclear reactor can drive steam turbines for months.

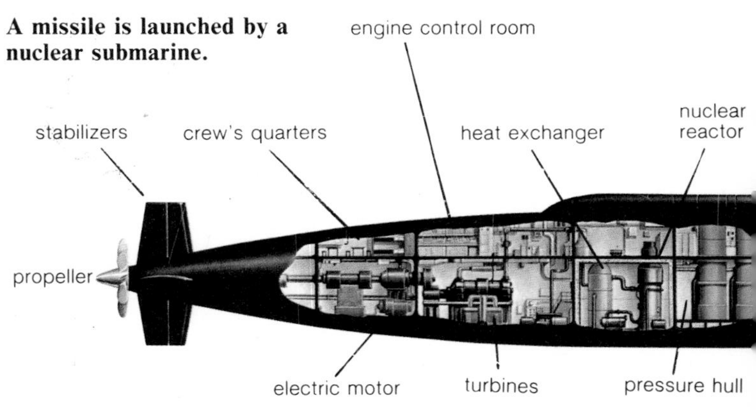

And it can do this without refueling.

The first nuclear submarine was the *Nautilus.* It was launched in 1954. It broke all underwater speed records. And in 1958 it traveled under the ice at the North Pole. Two years later the nuclear submarine *Triton* traveled all the way around the world. During the trip it never came to the surface. The voyage lasted for 84 days.

Nuclear Navies

Five navies have nuclear submarines. These are the navies of the United States, the Soviet Union, China, France, and Great Britain. Many nuclear submarines carry long-range missiles. The missiles can hit targets 4,000 miles (6,400 km) away. The newest American submarines carry Trident missiles. Each submarine has 24. One submarine could cause more destruction than all the fleets of World War II.

Some nuclear submarines are armed with new kinds of torpedoes. They are used to attack both enemy surface ships and submarines.

Life Beneath the Sea

A nuclear submarine has a crew of 150. An attack submarine goes to sea for six months. A missile submarine goes to sea for two months. It stays underwater the whole time. When it returns to its base, a new crew takes over. Then it goes to sea for another two months.

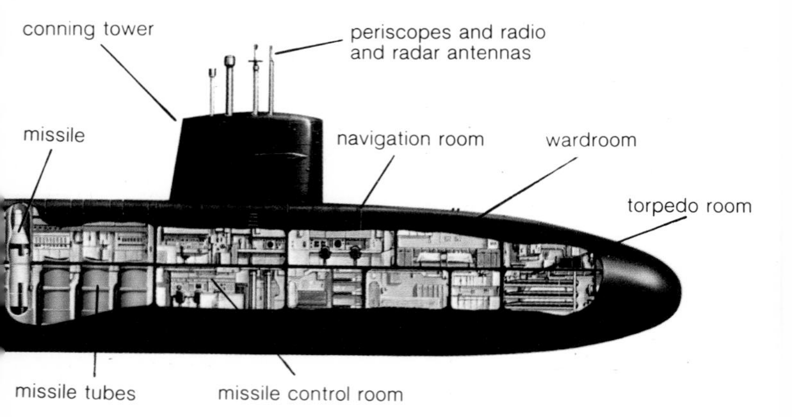

Deep Divers

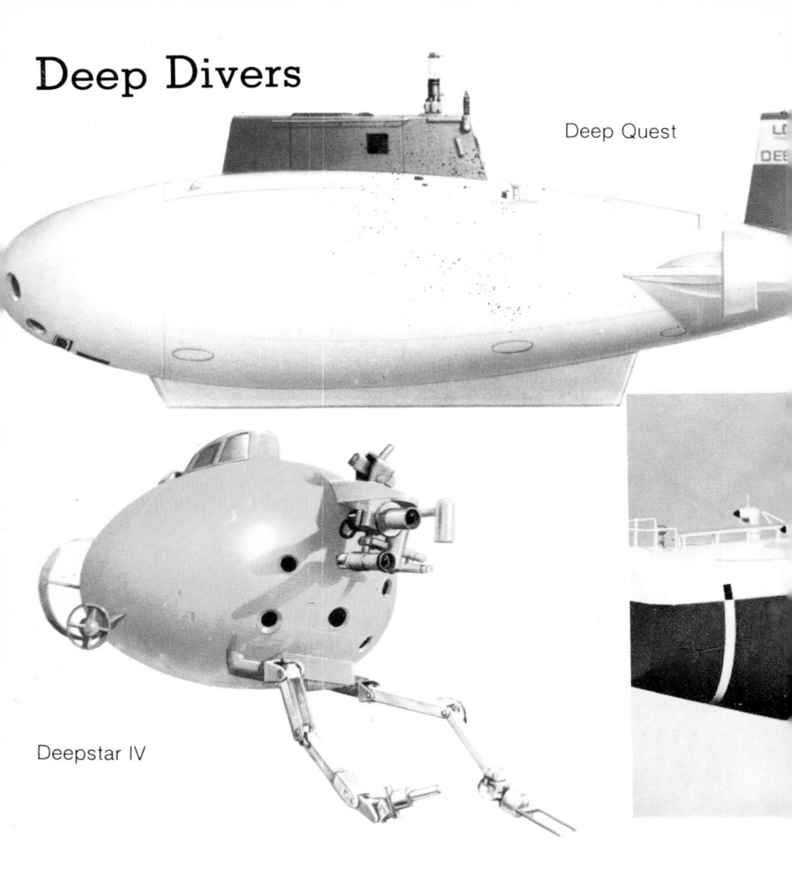

Deep Quest

Deepstar IV

The undersea world is the earth's last frontier. It can only be explored by submersible craft. Deep in the ocean, the water pressure is very great. So these craft must be very strong.

Early explorers of the ocean floor used armored diving suits and diving bells. They could only peer out and hope to see something interesting.

Ocean Rovers

Modern submersibles move under their own power. They can explore the bottom of the ocean more freely. The deepest dive of all was made in the *Trieste*. The *Trieste* is a bathyscaphe, a special diving craft used to explore the depths of the ocean. In 1960 the *Trieste* went down to the Challenger Deep in the Mar-

DIVING DEPTHS

(1) conventional submarine 500 feet (152 m)

(2) *Deepstar IV* 3,900 feet (1,189 m)

(3) *Deep Quest* 8,200 feet (2,500 m)

(4) *Aluminaut* 14,760 feet (4,500 m)

(5) *Trieste* 35,800 feet (10,915 m)

Trieste

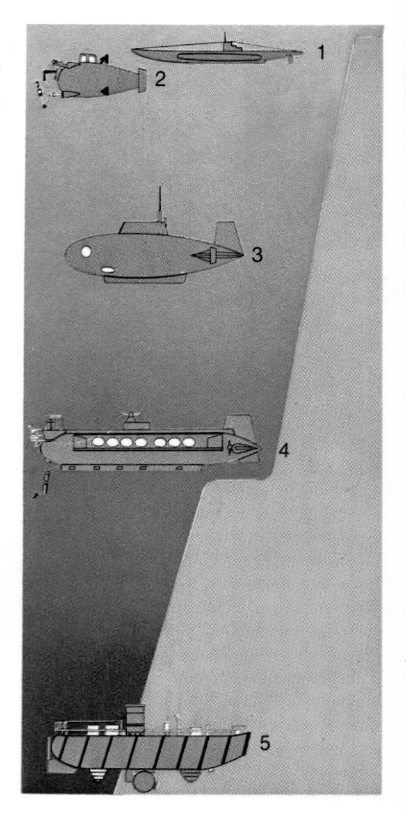

ianas Trench. This is the deepest part of the Pacific Ocean. It is 35,800 feet (10,915 m) below the surface.

The bathyscaphe is rather like a deep-sea airship. Its hull is filled with oil. (Oil is lighter than water.) It carries iron ballast. This enables it to dive. To return to the surface, it drops the ballast.

Deepstar IV and *Deep Quest* are smaller than *Trieste.* They are used to explore too. They are also used to help rescue submarines and to repair oil rigs.

One day there may be as many submersibles as there are surface ships. Today a "mother ship" has to carry the submersible to the diving site. In the future these deep-sea craft may use permanent undersea bases.

Ships of Today

The late 1800s and the early 1900s were a golden age for ships. Great advances were made. The screw propeller replaced paddle wheels. Then twin-screw propellers began to be used. These gave ships even greater power and speed. New types of engines, the steam turbine and the diesel engine, were built. These engines were powerful, and they used less fuel. This left more room for cargo. Ships became stronger with the use of steel. All of these improvements made it possible to build bigger and faster ships.

A recent development is the nuclear-powered merchant ship. The first one, the *Savannah*, was built in the United States. But it was taken out of service in 1971. West Germany, Japan, and the Soviet Union now have nuclear-powered ships. But they are expensive to build. And operating costs are high. Thus, most ships today use the cheaper diesel engines.

The Modern Liner

The largest passenger liners today are the *Queen Elizabeth 2* and the *Norway*. (The *Norway*'s original name was *France*.) These ships were built as transatlantic liners, but they now spend most of

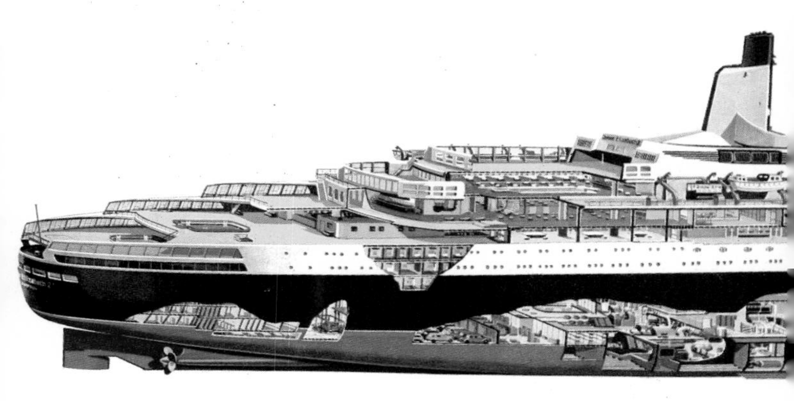

The *Queen Elizabeth 2* has all the luxuries of a first-class hotel.

their time on cruises. Some of the cruises are to the West Indies. Such a cruise may take only a few days. Sometimes these ships travel around the world, stopping at several continents. A trip like this takes months.

These beautiful floating hotels are well equipped for long voyages. This is what the *Queen Elizabeth 2,* (the *QE 2*) has to offer.

There is a playroom for children and a kennel for dogs and cats. There is a library and a theater. There are swimming pools, shops, and lounges. There are three dining rooms for the 2,000 passengers. And for after-dinner entertainment, there is a nightclub.

The *QE2* can cruise along at 28.5 knots (52.8 km/h). If there are rough seas, you won't feel them. The *QE2* has special gyroscopes. They keep the ship from rolling.

The Supertankers

The *Norway* is the largest liner afloat today. She is 1,035 feet (315.5 m) long. But she is dwarfed by the supertankers. Some of these giant ships are more than 1,500 feet (457 m) long. They are 200 feet (61 m) feet wide. And they can carry more than 500,000 tons of oil or other liquids. This is enough oil to fill the gas tanks of 14 million cars.

Despite their size these giant ships have crews of only fifty people. That is because they are controlled by computers. Computer control is necessary. A supertanker needs several miles of sea room to stop. The risk of a collision is everpresent. The oil spill from a collision can cause terrible damage.

Growth of the Tanker

The first tankers were built in the 1870s. The *Vaderland* was built in 1872. She was meant to carry both passengers and oil. But this was dangerous. The *Gluckauf* was built in 1886. She set the pattern for future tankers. Her engines were in the stern. This was as far away from the oil as possible.

During the 1900s, more and more countries switched from coal to oil. This increased the demand for oil. To carry more oil, people began to make bigger tankers. Much oil is sent from the Middle East to Europe, Japan, and the United States. The oil traveled in tankers

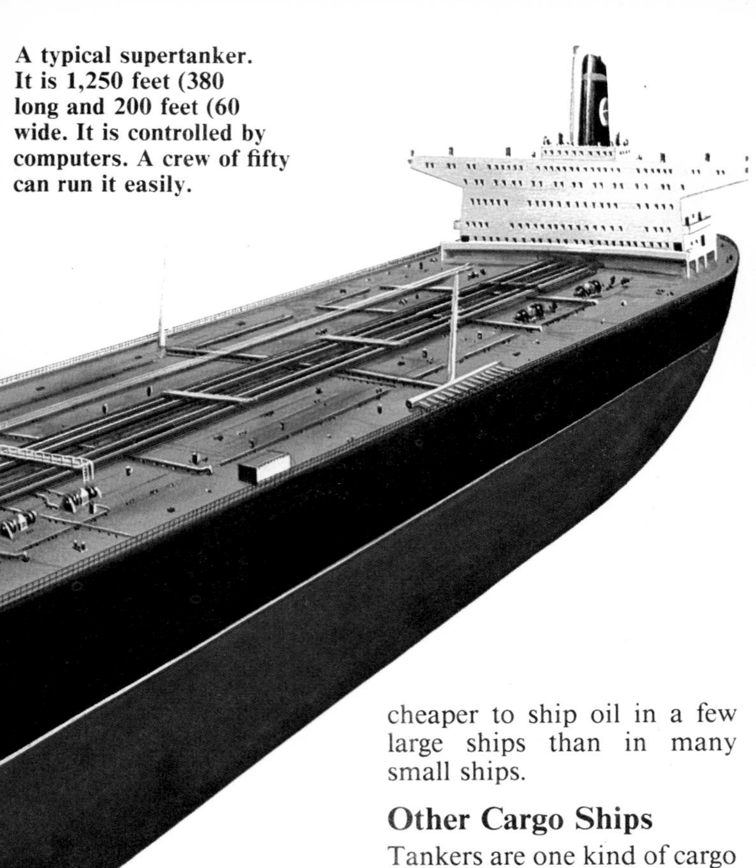

A typical supertanker. It is 1,250 feet (380 long and 200 feet (60 wide. It is controlled by computers. A crew of fifty can run it easily.

through the Suez Canal. But the Suez Canal was closed from 1967 to 1975. Oil then had to be shipped around the southern tip of Africa to get to Europe. For this long trip, shipbuilders began to make the supertankers. It was much cheaper to ship oil in a few large ships than in many small ships.

Other Cargo Ships

Tankers are one kind of cargo ship. There are three other kinds. Dry bulk carriers transport grain, coal, ore, and other dry cargoes. Some of these ships are giants too. They can carry more than 100,000 tons of cargo. General cargo ships carry such things as food, steel, motor vehicles, and machines. Multipurpose cargo ships carry many different kinds of cargo.

Heavyweights

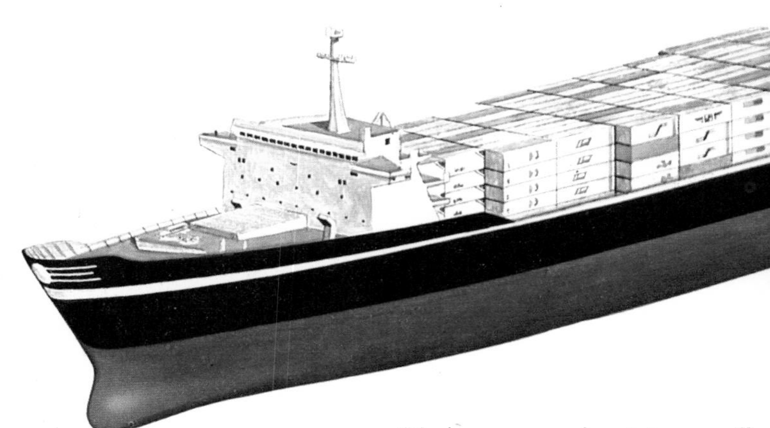

There is a reason why the supertankers are so big. Oil is a one-way cargo. After the tanker unloads its oil, it must make its return trip empty. So the bigger the ship, the cheaper the trip. Other bulk cargoes, such as iron ore, are also shipped in giant ships. Some special bulk carriers and container ships are almost as big as the supertankers.

Today the Suez Canal is deep enough to take many of these big ships. But the largest ones must make the long haul around Africa.

Loading and Unloading

Many of these superships are too big for docks and piers. They anchor in deep water. Their cargo is taken off through pipes or loaded into lighters (barges). LASH vessels can take the lighters on board. (LASH stands for "lighter-aboard-ship.") They do this by partly flooding their hulls. At the next port the barges float off again. Then they deliver the cargo by river and canal.

Money is saved if a cargo is loaded quickly. Today cargoes are rarely loaded bale by bale. Instead, truckloads may be driven straight on board. Or the cargo may arrive already packed inside special containers. Huge gantry cranes stack the containers onto the waiting ship. Container ships are fast and efficient.

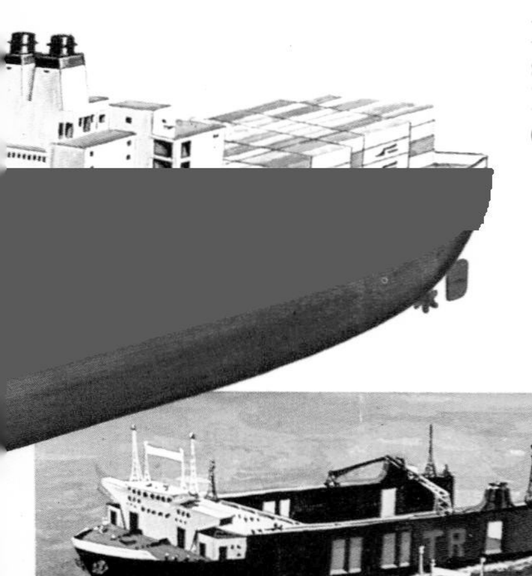

Left: A fully loaded container ship. It is 955 feet (291 m) long. It has a speed of 28 knots (52 km/h).

Below: A LASH ship. It lowers its hull into the water. The cargo floats aboard. A barge can also float aboard to be loaded.

Freighters and tankers are usually measured in *deadweight* tonnage. The tonnage is the weight of everything the ship can carry. It includes cargo, crew, fuel, and supplies.

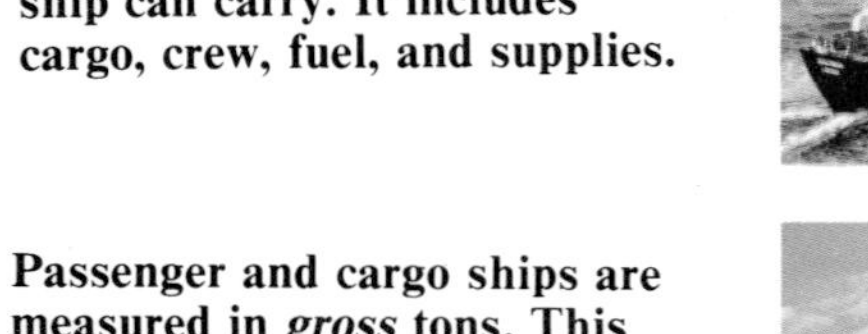

Passenger and cargo ships are measured in *gross* tons. This is a measure of volume (in units of 100 cubic feet). A 60,000-ton ship has 6 million cubic feet of space.

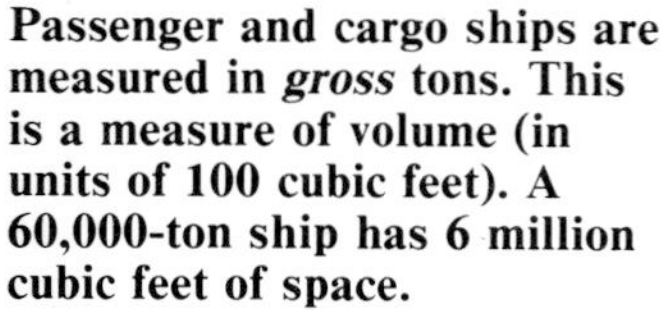

Warships are measured in *displacement* tonnage. This is the weight of water displaced by the ship.

Special Ships

The great cruise liners may be the queens of the sea. And the supertankers may be the stars. But there are other ships that are just as important.

Icebreakers and Tugboats

Polar waters are kept safe by icebreakers. The hull of an icebreaker is very strong. The ship must be able to resist the ice around it. The bow is specially shaped too. This is so the ship can ride up on top of the ice to crack it. If an icebreaker gets stuck, it can rock from side to side. This is done by pumping water back and forth between its ballast tanks. Most icebreakers also have bow propellers. These are used to draw the crushed ice away to the stern.

The tug is another workhorse. Tugs move big ships in and out of harbor. They carry out salvage work, and they tow big barges. Sometimes they help fight oil spills. Many tugs carry detergent sprays and oil-skimming booms.

Workhorses of the Sea

There are many other kinds of useful craft. They can be seen hard at work on the seas and on inland waterways.

Fishing vessels come in all sizes. Small ones fish along the coast. Giant fishing boats act as freeze trawlers and factory ships. Dredges keep river mouths and harbors free of silt. Oceangoing dredges mine the ocean floor. Research ships study the deep ocean. Weather ships watch for storms.

The FLIP research ship is the strangest ship of all. It can stand on end, becoming an underwater laboratory.

Above: A giant seagoing dredge. It is used to mine the seabed. The long boom gets rid of the waste.

Right: The FLIP research ship. It looks like a normal ship until it reaches its destination. Then it flips on its end, stern up.

Below: A tug at work. Large ships often need tugs to move them in and out of busy harbors.

Technology Afloat

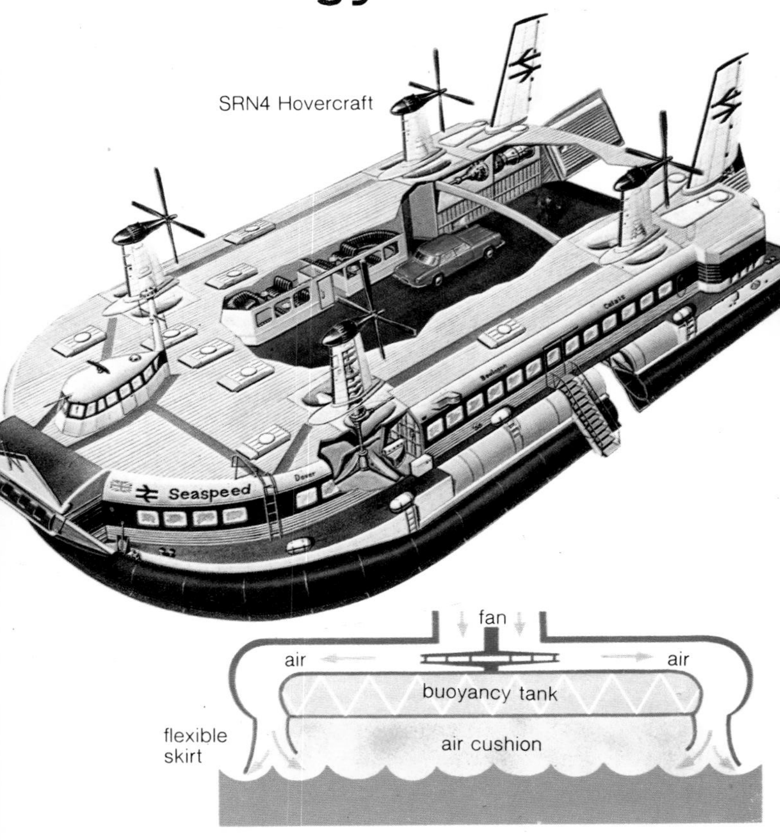

Not all seacraft float. Some skim on or just above the water. This cuts down on water resistance. Since water is denser than air, it exerts more drag on a ship's hull. Basically, this is why ships are slower than cars or planes.

Hovercraft float on a cushion of air. The SRN4 is an English Channel ferry.

Cushion Riders

One way to make a ship faster is to raise the hull off the water. The hovercraft rides

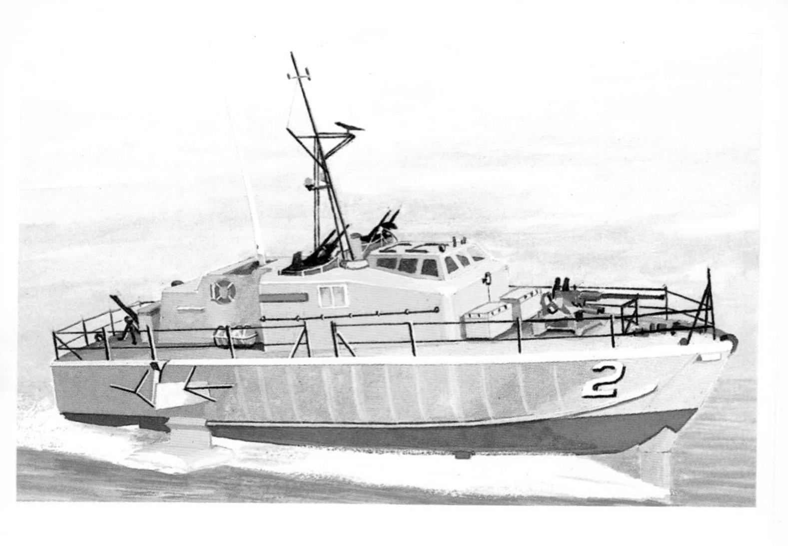

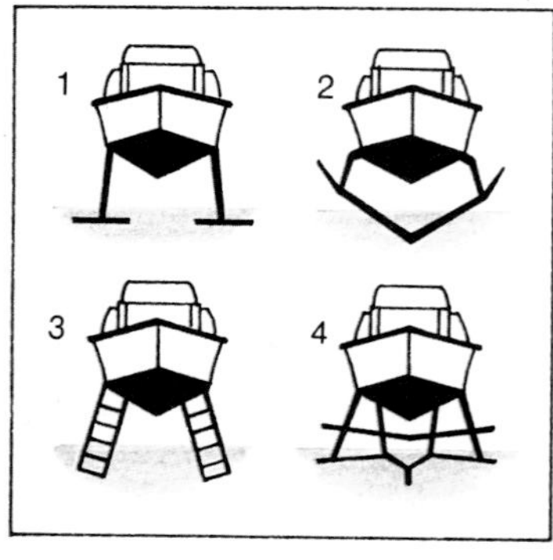

Above: A fast hydrofoil. Left: Four foil shapes—(1) submerged; (2) vee; (3) ladder; (4) shallow.

above the water. it was invented in the 1950s. It rides on a cushion of air. The air is blown downward by fans and is kept under the craft by flexible "skirts."

A craft with flexible skirts can also travel over land. This is why hovercraft make excellent ferries.

Surface Skimmers

At slow speeds, hydrofoils float like ordinary craft. When a hydrofoil speeds up, the hull lifts up on struts or foils. The hydrofoil then skims across the water.

Enrico Forlanini of Italy built the first successful hydrofoil. In 1906 it reached a speed of 36 knots (66.7 km/h). Modern hydrofoils are driven by water jets called jetfoils. They are the fastest passenger watercraft. Some can speed along at almost 50 knots (90 km/h).

Safety at Sea

Lightships like the one above are giving way to large radio buoys.

Seafarers face many dangers—rocks and reefs, storms and fog. Today ships have modern navigational equipment. But even so, more than 100 ships are lost at sea each year. And many times that number of small craft are lost.

Lights and Buoys

The first lighthouses were built in ancient times. They warned ships of dangerous rocks and currents. The lighthouse at Alexandria, Egypt, was one of the Seven Wonders of the World.

The first modern style of lighthouse was built in 1759. It was built on Eddystone Rock. It stands off the coast of Plymouth, England. Today coastal light towers are a familiar sight. Their flashing beacons have saved many ships. Far from the shore, lightships and navigation buoys are used. Their light can be seen from a distance of 12 miles (20 km). Small buoys are anchored to mark underwater obstacles.

Lifeboats

In 1789 a ship named the *Adventure* was wrecked off the English coast. it was less than 1,000 feet (300 m) from shore. A crowd of people watched helplessly. No boat could reach the doomed ship.

The next year a competition was held. People were asked to design a lifeboat. Henry Greathead's *Original* was the winner. She was 33 feet (10 m) long. She had cork at the bow and stern for extra buoyancy.

In 1824 the Royal National Lifeboat Institution was founded in Great Britain. Other countries quickly followed this example. Today lifeboats are used around the world.

The *Original* had only oars. Modern lifeboats are diesel-powered. The largest ones are "self-righting." If one of these boats turns over, it will automatically right itself again. Water ballast shifts from one tank to another. It brings the boat upright in seven seconds. Small inflatable craft are used for rescues close to shore.

Modern lifeboats are about 50 feet (15m) long. They are designed for strength. They must withstand a pounding from the heaviest waves.

Oil Rigs

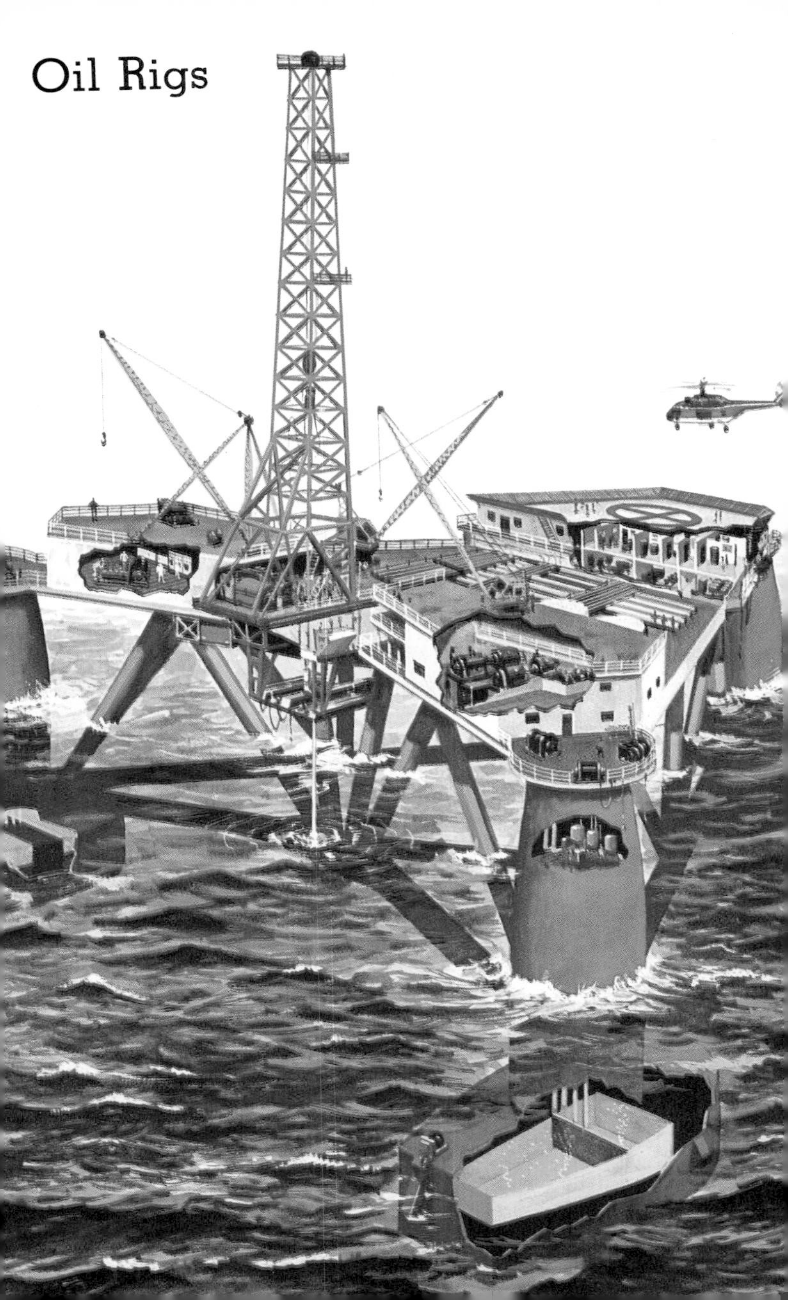

This drilling rig is specially equipped to fight fires at sea.

In some places oil seeps to the surface through cracks in the ground. In other places, such as deserts, it lies far below the surface. But it is most difficult to get at oil when it is below the bottom of the sea. Huge platforms and drilling rigs must be built. Then they must be towed out to sea.

Three kinds of drilling rigs are shown below. Early rigs sat on the seabed. They had fixed platforms and could not be moved. On a *jack-up rig* the legs can be raised and the rig towed to a new site. The *semisubmersible floating rig* (see picture opposite) is used in very deep water. It is floated out to the drilling site. The floats in its legs are then partly flooded. The rig is half submerged and anchored in place.

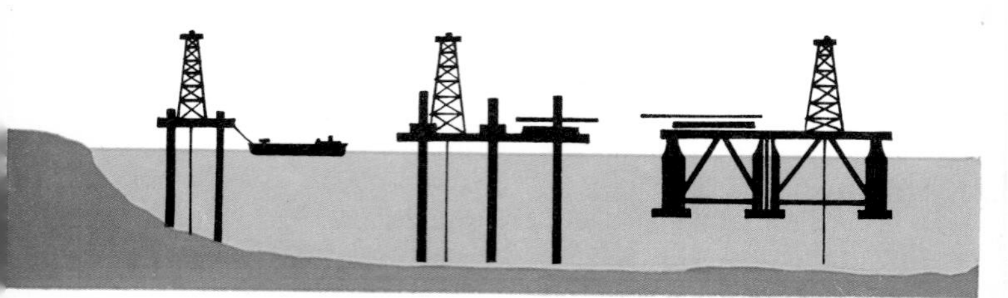

Below (left to right): fixed platform; movable jack-up rig; semisubmersible rig.

More Facts

How are ships built? How are they navigated? What will ships of the future look like? These and many other questions are answered in this fact-filled section. You will learn more about sailing ships. You will meet some strange ships and some lost ships—and some treasure ships.

FOUR STAGES IN BUILDING A SHIP

1

2

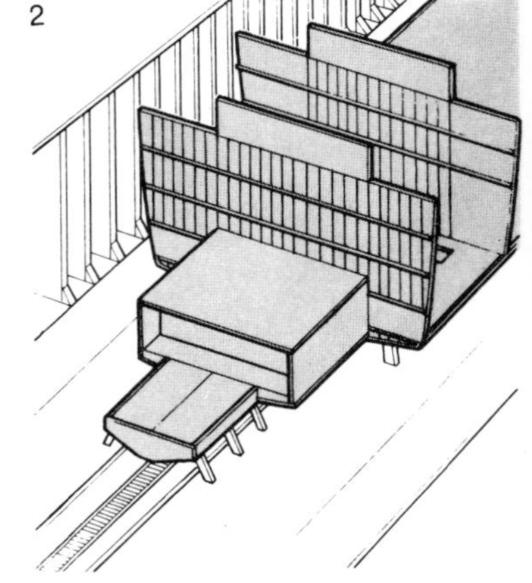

1. Modern ships are built in sections. Here the first stage of welded plating is laid over the keel.

2. The main watertight bulkheads are in place. Steel plates are traced and cut with electronic accuracy.

Shipbuilding

Until the 1800s, all ships were built of wood. The people who built them were called shipwrights. They worked in shipyards. Shipwrights rarely used scale models or plans until the 1700s. In fact, they rarely used accurate measurements.

With the Industrial Revolution came iron and steel ships. Shipbuilding became an industry. Even then, the method of making ships did not change very much. First the keel was laid. Then a framework of ribs was added. This was followed by beams and girders for the decks. Lastly the outer skin of metal plates was riveted in place. (Later the plates would be welded.)

At her launching the *Great Eastern* was pushed sideways into the Thames River. Most modern ships are launched stern first, at high tide.

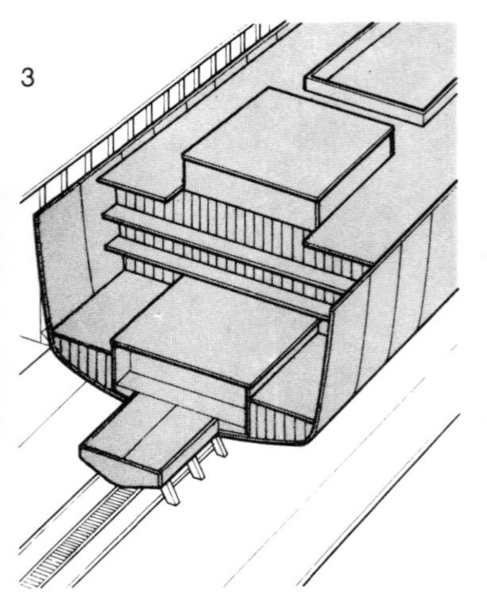

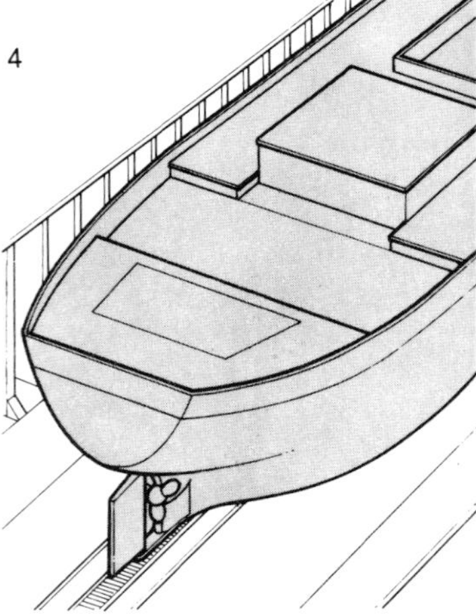

3. The builders work from a 1/10 scale plan. They add the decks and side plates. The ship begins to take shape.

4. Curved stern plates are added, bent to shape by computer-guided hydraulic presses. The hull is now nearly completed.

Navigation

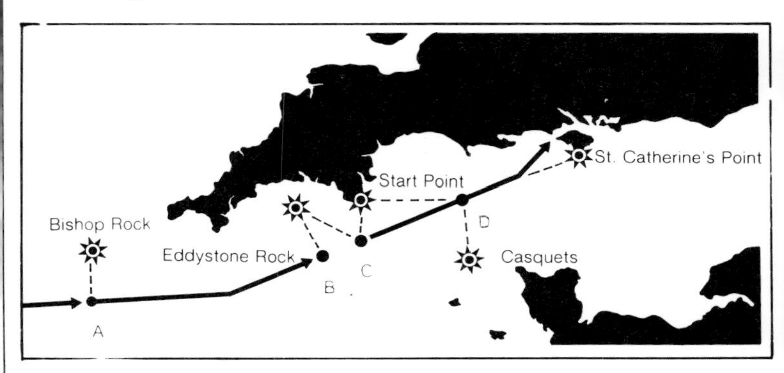

More and more, electronics are taking over the ship at sea.

At points A, B, C, and D, a ship sailing east up the English Channel can fix its position from shore landmarks.

Automatic Pilots

A human pilot is still needed to guide a big ship through crowded coastal waters and into port. But at sea the captain turns on the ship's automatic pilot. Gyrocompasses reflect the smallest changes in course, and the rudder is corrected automatically.

Radar scanners keep watch for other vessels. Direction finders receive signals from shore transmitters. Echo-sounding sonar pulses are beamed down. They measure the depth of the water beneath the ship. The ship's position may then be shown on a computerized map.

Dead Reckoning

To learn the ship's position, or *fix,* the navigator must know its latitude and longitude. (Latitude is the distance north or south of the equator. Longitude is the distance east or west of a known point—usually the prime meridian at Greenwich, England.) In terms of dead reckoning, the navigator charts the last known point of latitude and longitude. Exact measurements of speed and course are noted. So are the distance traveled and the time since the last fix. Corrections are made for wind and ocean currents. From all this information the navigator calculates a new fix. Nowadays many ships at sea are guided by space satellites rather than dead reckoning.

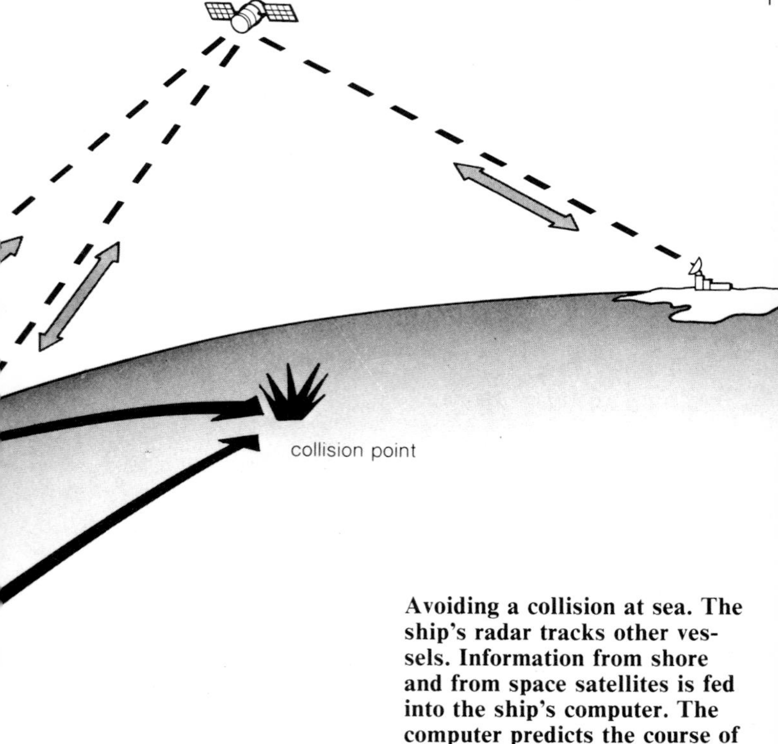

Avoiding a collision at sea. The ship's radar tracks other vessels. Information from shore and from space satellites is fed into the ship's computer. The computer predicts the course of nearby vessels. The ship can change course to avoid collision.

Docks

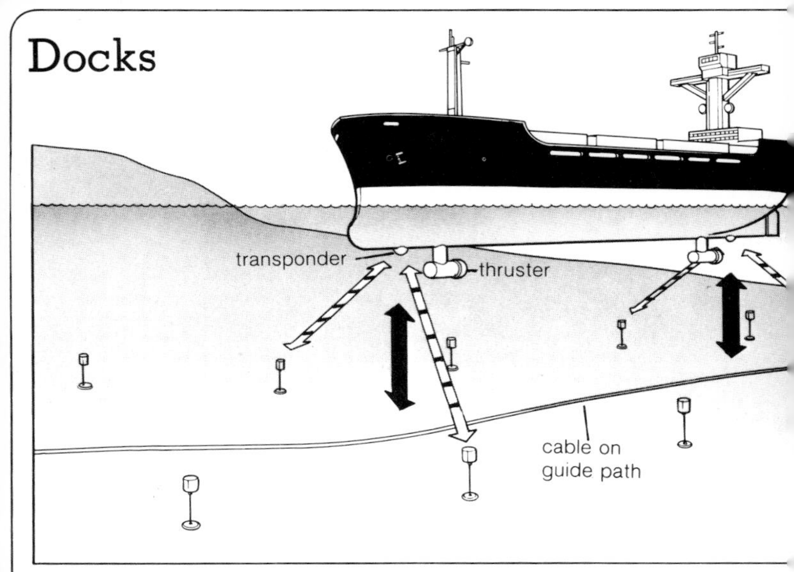

A ship ties up at a dock to load or unload its cargo. In the past, tall cranes lifted boxes of cargo off the ship. Today a more familiar sight is the gantry. These are special platforms that carry huge cranes. Enormous containers can be lifted off the waiting ships.

MAJOR PORTS
Rotterdam, Netherlands
New York City
San Francisco
London, United Kingdom
Hamburg, West Germany
Yokohama, Japan
Buenos Aires, Argentina
Rio de Janeiro, Brazil
Bombay, India
Shanghai, China
Singapore, Singapore

Special Cargoes

Some cargoes are handled in special ways. Liquids are pumped from the ship into storage tanks. Grain is sucked into giant silos. And conveyor belts whisk frozen meats and perishable fruit into giant refrigerators.

Oil tankers and tankers that carry liquefied natural gas usually berth far offshore at jetties. From there the cargo is piped to the land.

Floating Docks

In some ways, ships are like cars. They need to be serviced regularly. They get serviced in a *dry dock*. A dry dock is like a garage. It is a concrete basin

An automatic guidance system for ships entering port. Transponders send signals. These tell the ship if it is over the guide path. The thrusters keep the ship on the right path.

moored transponders
at edge of guide path

with watertight gates. The ship floats into the dry dock. Then the gates are shut and the water is pumped out. The ship is left "high and dry." It can now be serviced.

Ships can also be serviced in a *floating dock.* A floating dock can be flooded to let the ship float inside. The water is then pumped out. When this is done, the dock rises. As it rises, it lifts the ship with it.

The conventional dry dock (below) is on land. The floating dry dock (bottom) handles ships in deep water.

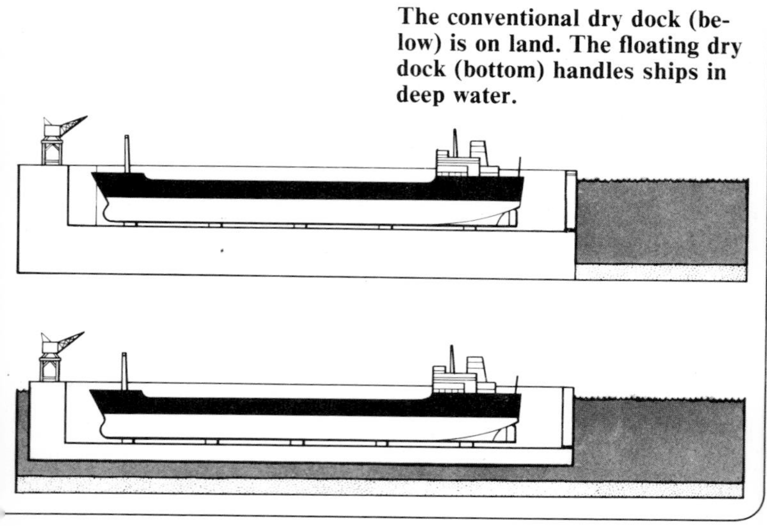

Ships at Work

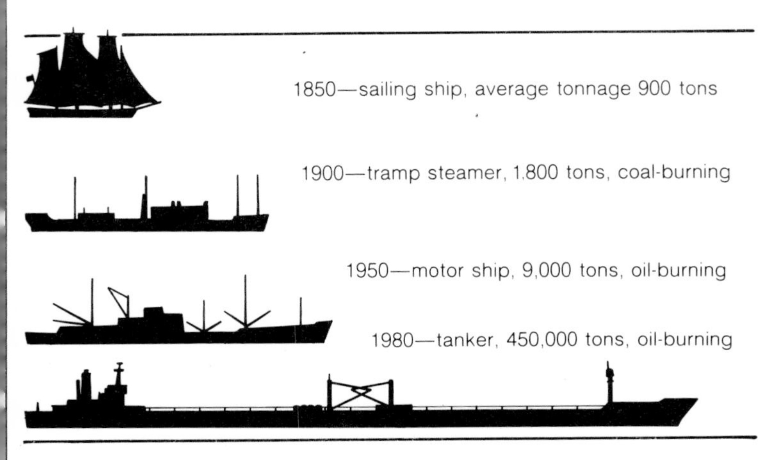

Above: This table shows how cargo ships became steadily bigger and more powerful.

There are more than 70,000 merchant ships in the world. The business of shipping cargo is very competitive. It was just the same in the days of sail. Then success depended on the skill of the captain. It also depended on the size and speed of the ship.

The era of sailing vessels ended in the 1880s. Steam vessels took over. They could go faster and carry more cargo. A tramp steamer of the early 1900s burned 17 tons of coal a day. Today a modern diesel-powered ship burns only 5 tons of oil a day. Yet it can carry twice the cargo. Huge tankers can carry more than half a million tons of cargo.

Working Under the Sea

A less familiar type of ship work is mining. Deepwater dredges suck up minerals from the ocean floor. They use a long hose or pipe to do this. At the end of the pipe is a sledgelike scoop. Another way to mine the ocean floor is to use a chain of buckets. But this is tricky in very deep water.

Mining ships have brought up manganese from a depth of more than 16,350 feet (5,000 m).

Right: A dredge sucks up manganese from the ocean floor.

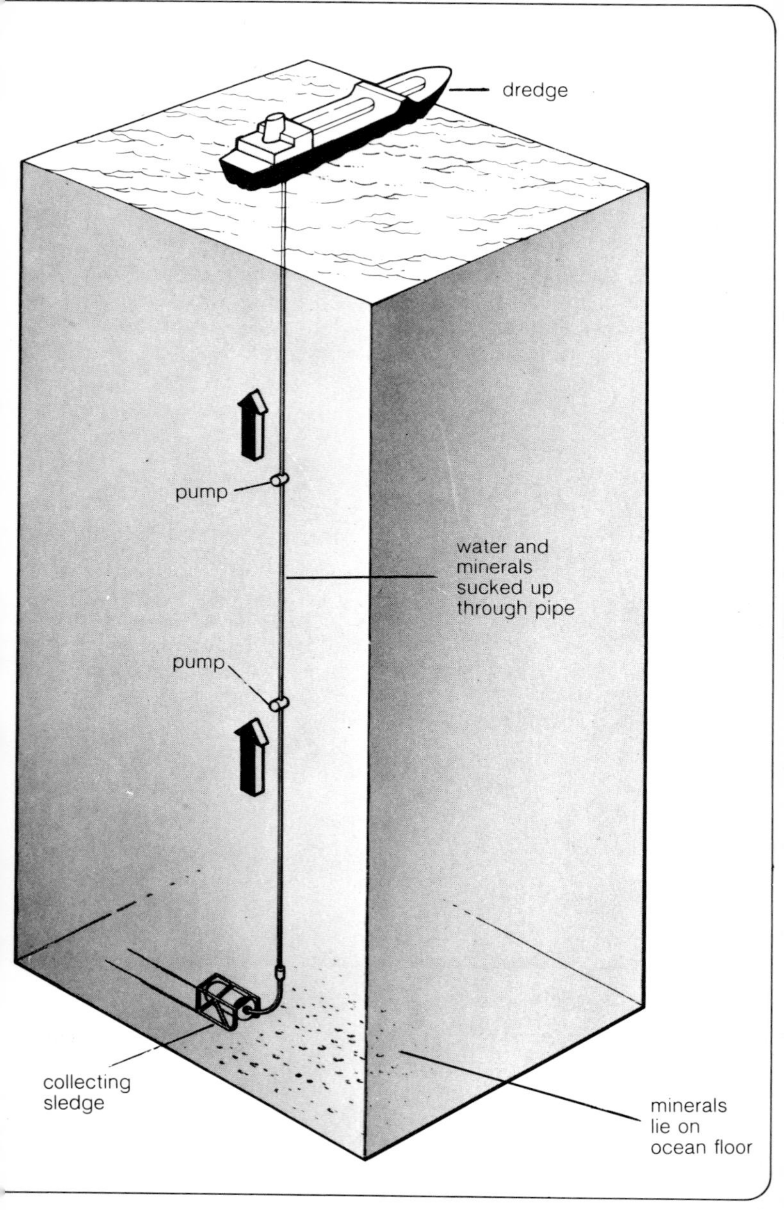
dredge
pump
water and
minerals
sucked up
through pipe
pump
collecting
sledge
minerals
lie on
ocean floor

Future Shapes

The oceans are rich in fish. There is animal life even on the deepest part of the seabed. There are also valuable minerals. Can people live and work at these great depths?

Today most submersibles can only explore to a little over 13,000 feet (4,000 m). So half of the seabed is beyond our reach. But in the next century there will be robot diving systems. And there will be deepwater nuclear-powered submarines. They will open up this new world. Perhaps an ocean-floor base like the one shown here will be built.

But on the surface, sails may make a comeback. Oil will be very scarce and costly. But wind power is free, and it will never run out. Fact or fiction? Only time will tell.

A look at the undersea world of the next century: (1) tourist "bus" submersible; (2) air lock entrance to seabed base; (3 and 4) seabed base in pressurized domes; (5) scuba diver checking equipment; (6) fish farm; (7) nuclear-powered "tug" sub, towing a cargo unit (8); (9) sail cargo ship, controlled by electronic robots and computers.

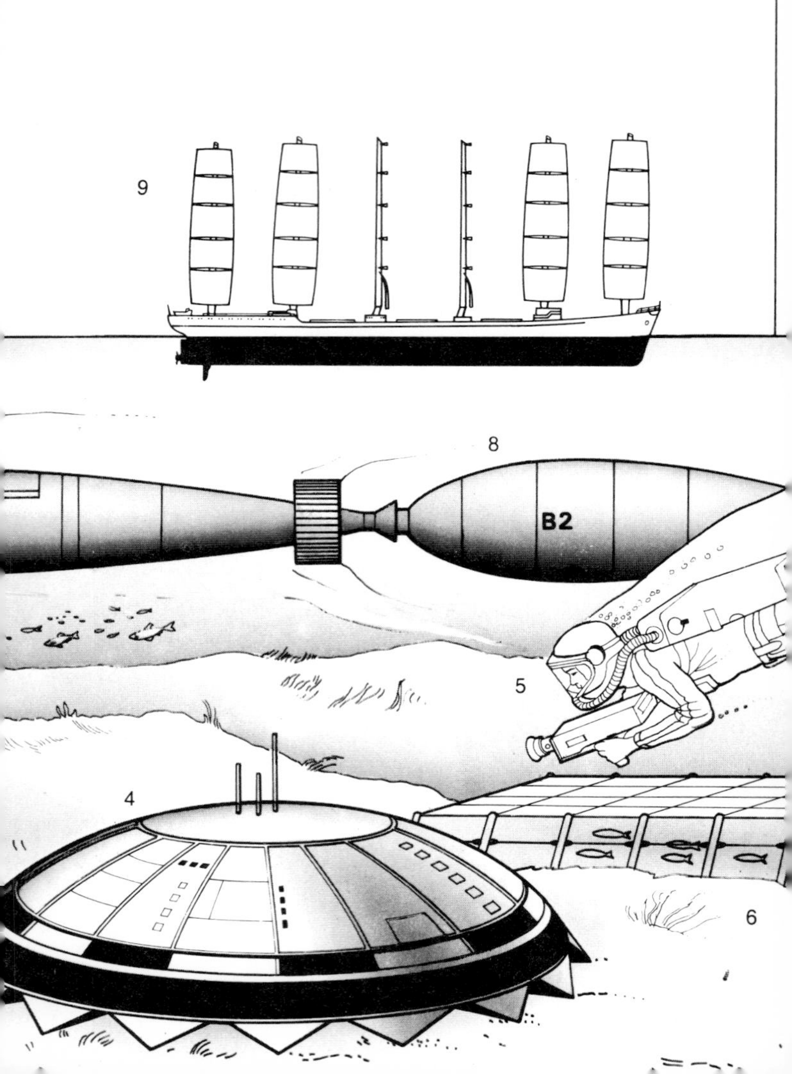

Future Power

Most ships are powered by steam turbines or diesel engines. Both types of engines use oil as a fuel. Oil is now expensive. As supplies shrink, it will become even more expensive. And some day there will be no more oil. Other forms of energy will have to be found.

The Nuclear Ship

In the 1950s nuclear power seemed to be the answer. It was tried in submarines. It was also tried in a few surface ships. The U.S. warship *Long Beach* and merchant ship *Savannah* were nuclear-powered. So were the Soviet icebreaker *Lenin* and the West German ship *Otto Hahn.*

How does a nuclear-powered ship work? Basically the atomic reactor produces heat energy. This energy drives steam turbines. A nuclear-powered ship can travel thousands of miles without refueling. But the costs are high, and now there are doubts about nuclear safety.

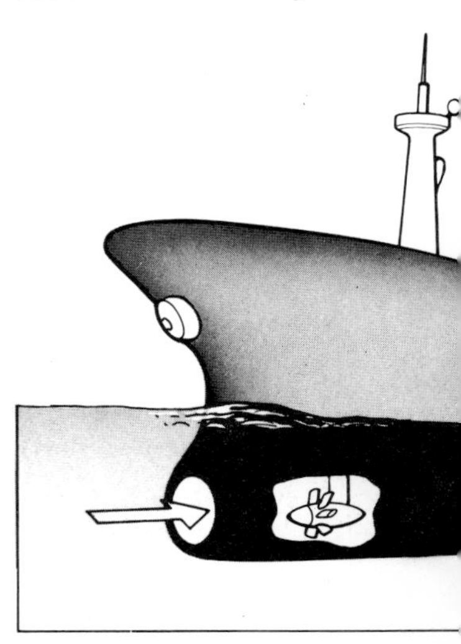

The Soviet icebreaker *Lenin* (1957). She was the first nuclear-powered surface ship.

Someday water jets may power big ships. Diesel-driven motors would speed up the water flow.

Coal, Sun, and Wind

What, then, will be used for fuel in the future? Coal could become cheaper than oil. And modern coal-burning ships would not need stokers to tend the furnaces. The process would be automatic. It could be done with computers.

Solar energy could be another solution. Solar energy uses the sun's rays to make electric power. This electric power could run the ships.

The oldest and cheapest source of power at sea is the wind. Speed is not important for some cargoes that have to travel great distances. Perhaps, for long-haul cargo, sailing ships might make a comeback.

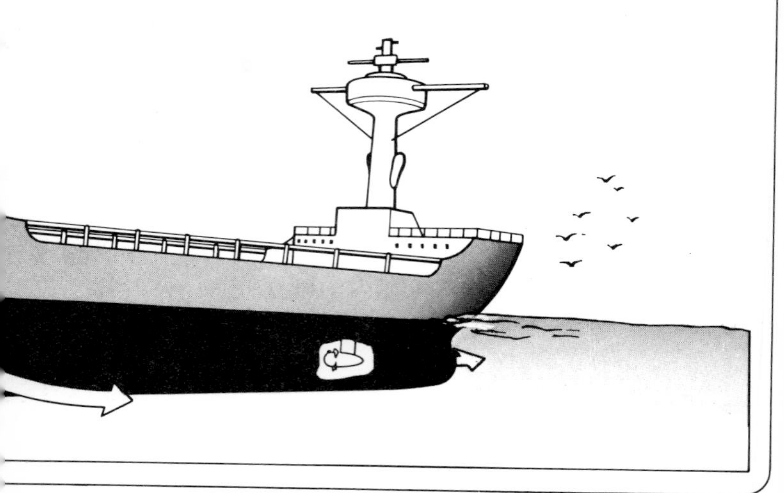

Sailing Craft

Today's sailing craft are quite different from those made in the past. Until the 1940s, no two ships were exactly the same. But then builders began to make sailing craft with water-resistant plywood and fiberglass. Anything from a tiny dinghy to an 18-meter yacht can be molded in fiberglass. Even sails are made from synthetic materials such as nylon and Dacron.

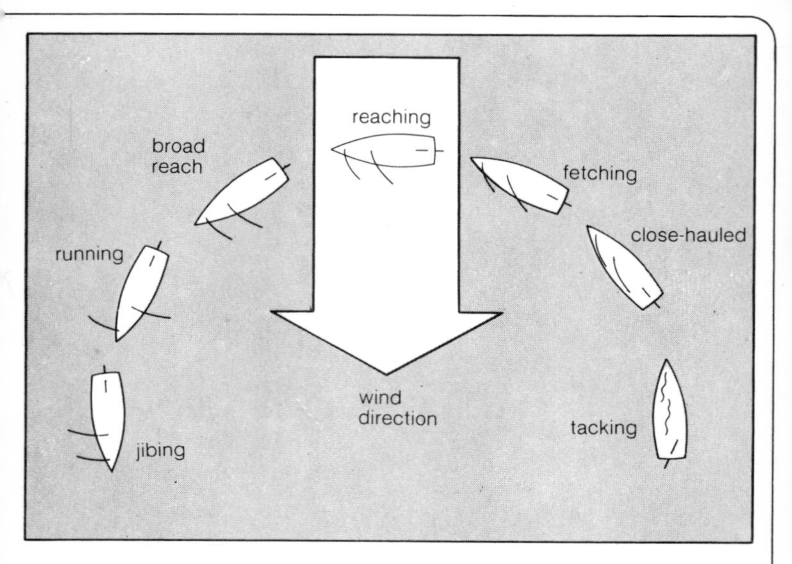

Left: Typical modern sailing craft—a small dinghy (top) and a catamaran.

Above: A sailing ship can sail "before the wind" or at various angles to it.

YACHTING WORDS

aft Toward the stern.
beam Width of a boat at its widest point.
boom A long spar that holds the foot of a sail.
centerboard A keel that can be raised and lowered through the bottom of a small boat.
cleat T-shaped fitting for fastening ropes.
forward Toward the bow
halyard A line for raising or lowering sails or flags.
leeward Away from the wind; downwind.
make fast To tie in place.
sheet A line used to trim a sail.
shroud A line or wire that supports the mast.
spinnaker Three-cornered sail set forward to increase total sail area.
tiller A lever used to move the rudder of a boat.
windward The direction from which the wind is blowing.

Sailing Rigs

brig

lateen

barkentine

brigantine

schooner

Sailing ships use many different sail arrangements. Some traditional rigs are shown here. There were two main types of rigs. One was the *lateen.* It used triangular sails. The other was the *ship rig,* or square rig. It used square sails.

The clippers and the windjammers were the last of the square-rigged sailing ships.

The *fore-and-aft rig* uses no square sails. A rig combining square and triangular sails was first used by the Dutch in the 1400s. It needed a smaller crew to work it. It became popular for small craft.

The barks and barkentines were three-masted ships. They also used a combination of square rigging and fore-and-aft rigging. So did the smaller two-masted brigs and brigantines.

lugger

cutter

bark

square-rigger

smack

SAILING RECORDS

The farthest day's run by a sailing ship was just under 536 miles (862 km). The clipper *Champion of the Seas* set this record.

Robin Knox-Johnson spent a record 312 days at sea in *Suhaili* (1968–69). He made the first nonstop solo trip around the world.

The fastest sailing merchantman was the windjammer *Lancing*—22 knots (40.7 km/h).

The ship with the most sails (63) was the East Indiaman *Essex*.

The largest sailing ship was *France II* (1911), at 417 feet (127 m).

Bizarre Ships

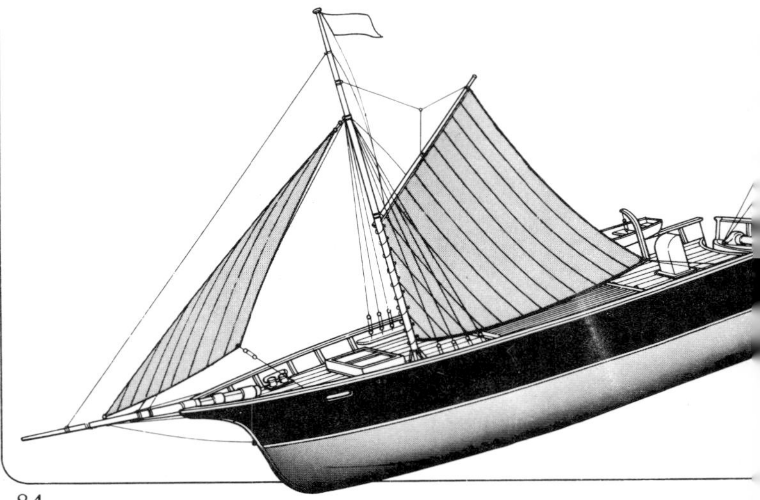

Left: The *Bessemer.* It was hoped the hydraulic design would prevent seasickness.

Above: Cleopatra's Needle is a huge stone obelisk. In 1887 it was shipped to London from Egypt. A prefabricated barge was rebuilt around the obelisk. Then it was towed to England.

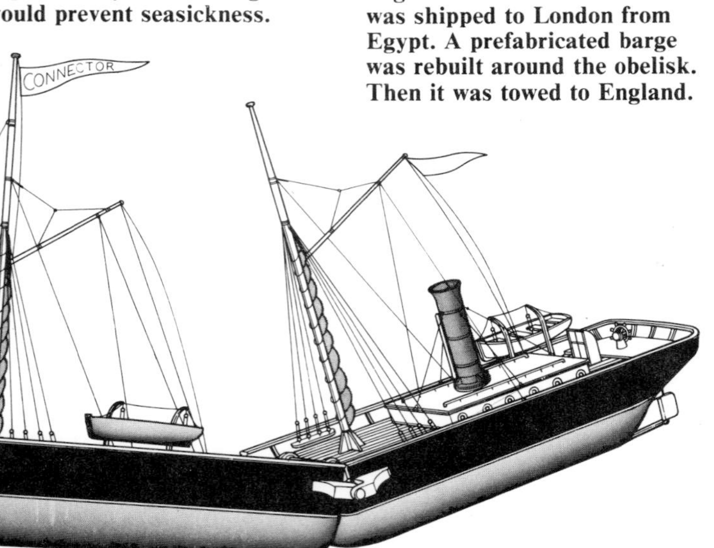

Above: The jointed *Connector.* The bow and midship cargo sections could be uncoupled from the stern engine section. Ready-loaded "spares" could then be hooked on at port.

Treasure Ships

Every year ships are lost at sea. Most are forgotten. But a few attract salvage teams and divers. Some people are drawn to the ships hoping to find sunken treasure. Others are attracted by the ships' historical interest.

Raising a Wreck

Some ships sink in shallow water. If the wreck is in one piece, it can sometimes be lifted. Cables are passed beneath it. It can then be lifted at high tide. Another way to lift a wreck is with air. The hull is made airtight. Then air is pumped in. The wreck rises like a balloon.

Lost Gold

The *San Josef* was a Spanish treasure galleon. In 1708 she was sunk by British warships. The wreck is thought to be off the coast of Colombia. The water there is hundreds of feet deep. The treasure on the ship is thought to be worth billions of dollars.

The *Laurentic* (1917), the *Egypt* (1922), and the *Edinburgh* (1942) all sank with gold on board. Divers have brought up most of this gold.

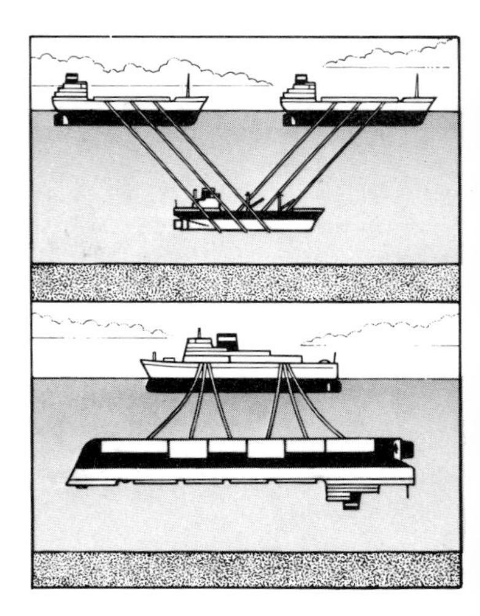

Sunken ships can be salvaged by cable lift (top) or air inflation (bottom).

The *Edinburgh* was a British cruiser. It sank in the freezing Barents Sea. It was carrying several tons of Russian gold. The salvagers received millions of dollars.

Preserving the Past

Archaeologists are more interested in lost ships than lost gold. The *Mary Rose* was one of the jewels of King Henry VIII's navy. She sank in 1545 off the southern coast of England. Her remains have been

The wreck of the *Mary Rose.* Its size is compared to that of a bus.

carefully raised to the surface. They are like a time capsule of Elizabethan life at sea. Everything that was on the *Mary Rose* will be studied.

The *Mary Rose* sank in the Solent. This is a channel between the Isle of Wight and southern England. The mud there preserved the ship. It will be possible to reconstruct life aboard a great galleon. We will learn about the "beste shippe within the realme," as the *Mary Rose* was proudly called.

FAMOUS WRECKS

Lutine (1799). Her bell now hangs in Lloyd's of London (the marine insurers).

Laurentic (1917). Sunk by a German mine. Divers recovered 3,186 of her 3,211 gold ingots.

Marie Celeste (1872). Found under sail but deserted in the Atlantic. There was no trace of her crew. In 1885 she was finally wrecked off Cuba.

Solo Sailors

Joshua Slocum was the first person to sail around the world alone. He did this between 1895 and 1898, in his yacht *Spray*. Hugo Vihlen sailed a tiny craft, *April Fool,* across the southern Atlantic in 1968. In 1982, Tom McClean's *Giltspur* and Bill Dunlop's *Wind's Will* made the northern crossing.

John Fairfax was the first to row across the Atlantic alone. He did it, east to west, in 180 days. Tom McClean rowed west to east in 70 days.

In 1974, Alain Colas made the fastest solo trip around the world—in a trimaran in 167 days. The official water speed record is 319 miles per hour (513 km/h). Ken Warby set it in 1977, in his hydroplane *Spirit of Australia.* Donald Campbell was a previous record holder. He was killed when his *Bluebird* crashed in 1967.

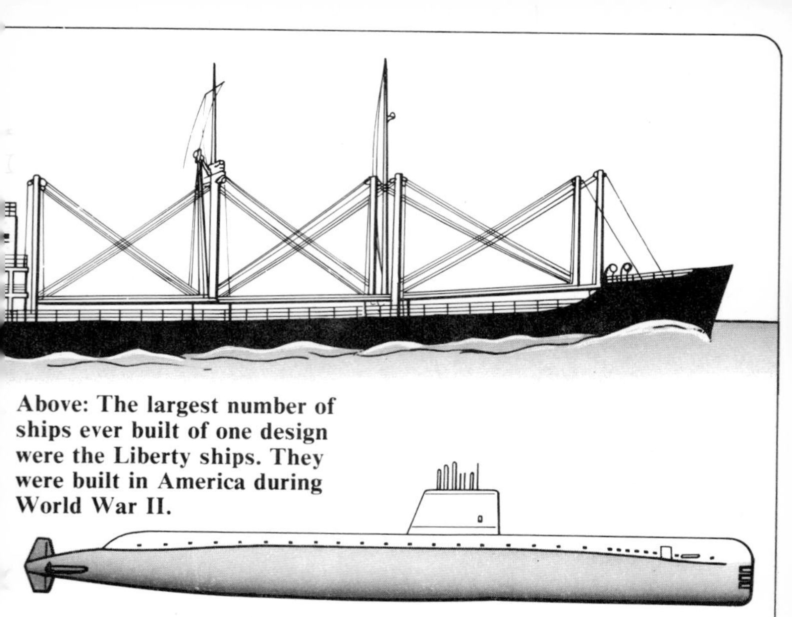

Above: The largest number of ships ever built of one design were the Liberty ships. They were built in America during World War II.

Left: Donald Campbell's *Bluebird.* This hydroplane broke the water speed record in 1967.

Above: The USS *Nautilus.* She was the world's first nuclear-powered submarine.

HEADLINE MAKERS

Largest The world's largest ship is the tanker *Seawise Giant* (1982). It is 1,504 feet (458.45 m) long. And it is 564,739 deadweight tons. The largest warship is the USS *Nimitz.* It is 1,092 feet (333 m) long. And it is over 96,000 tons fully loaded.
Fastest The U.S. Navy hovercraft SES-100B has reached 91 knots (168 km/h). Hydrofoils can go faster than 60 knots (111 km/h). The liner *United States* has a top speed of 41.75 knots (77 km/h).
Worst Disaster The German ship *Wilhelm Gustaf* was torpedoed in January 1945. At least 5,800 died.

Battle Group

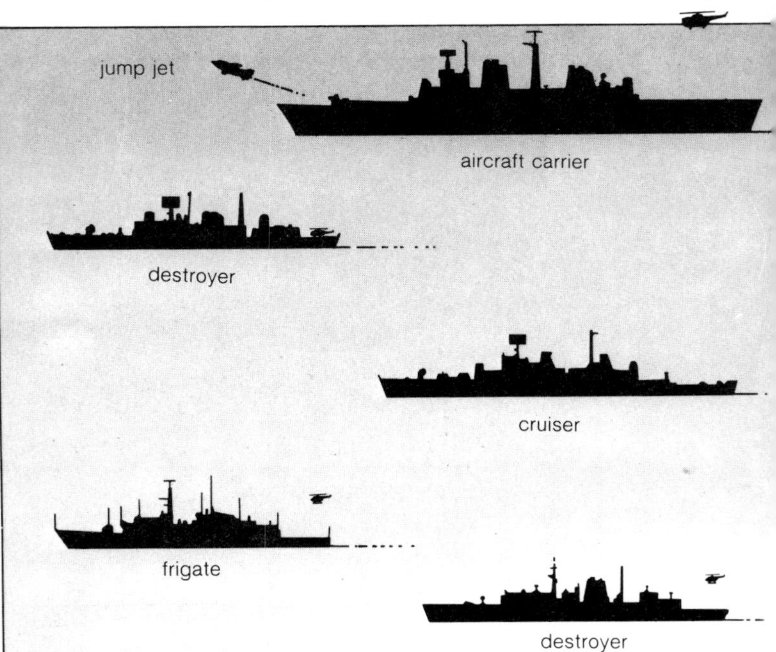

There are many different kinds of ships in a battle group. These ships cruise together for protection.

The fleet has two very dangerous enemies. Submarines are a threat. So are long-range missiles launched from aircraft. Early-warning aircraft warn the fleet if an enemy approaches. United States' early-warning aircraft are called AWACS. British planes of this type are called Nimrod.

Small aircraft carriers can carry jump jets. These planes can take off from short decks. Helicopters are attached to battle groups. Frigates and destroyers carry them. These ships are also heavily armed with missiles, torpedoes, and guns.

In war, a battle group would protect convoys that are ferrying troops and supplies. It could also launch a major landing.

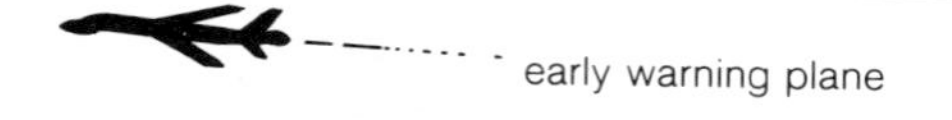
early warning plane

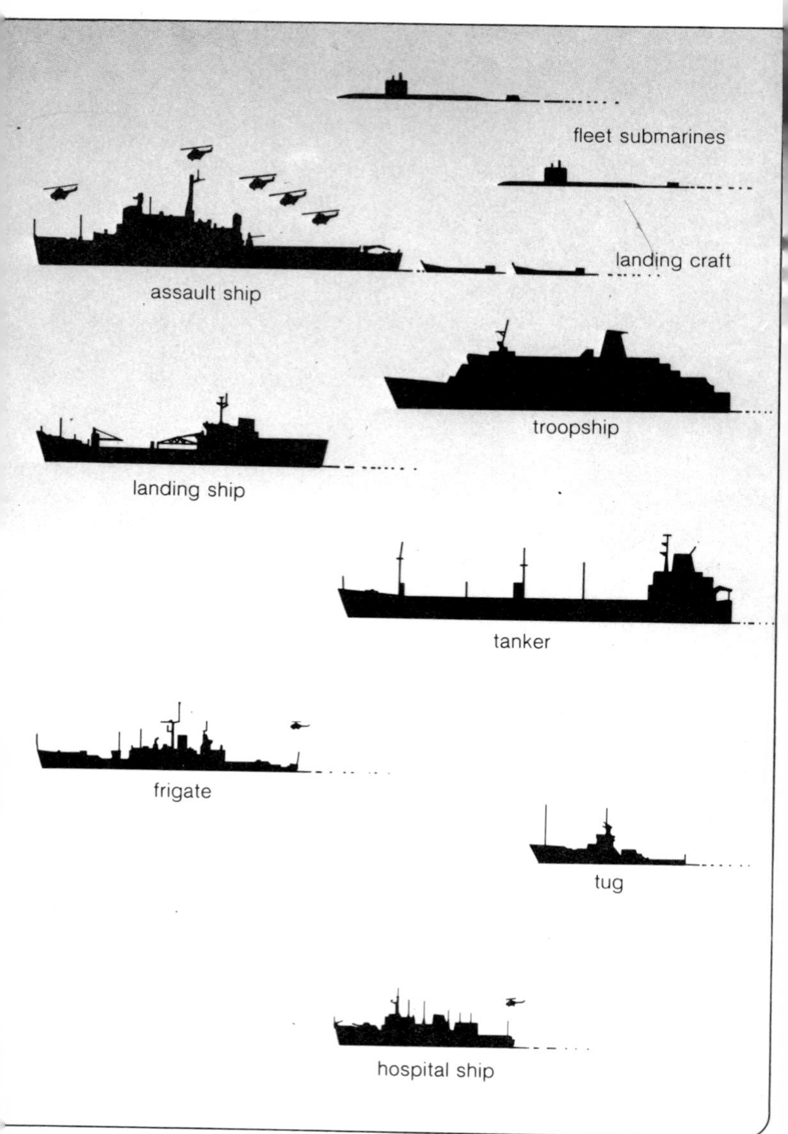
fleet submarines
landing craft
assault ship
troopship
landing ship
tanker
frigate
tug
hospital ship

Index

early warning plane

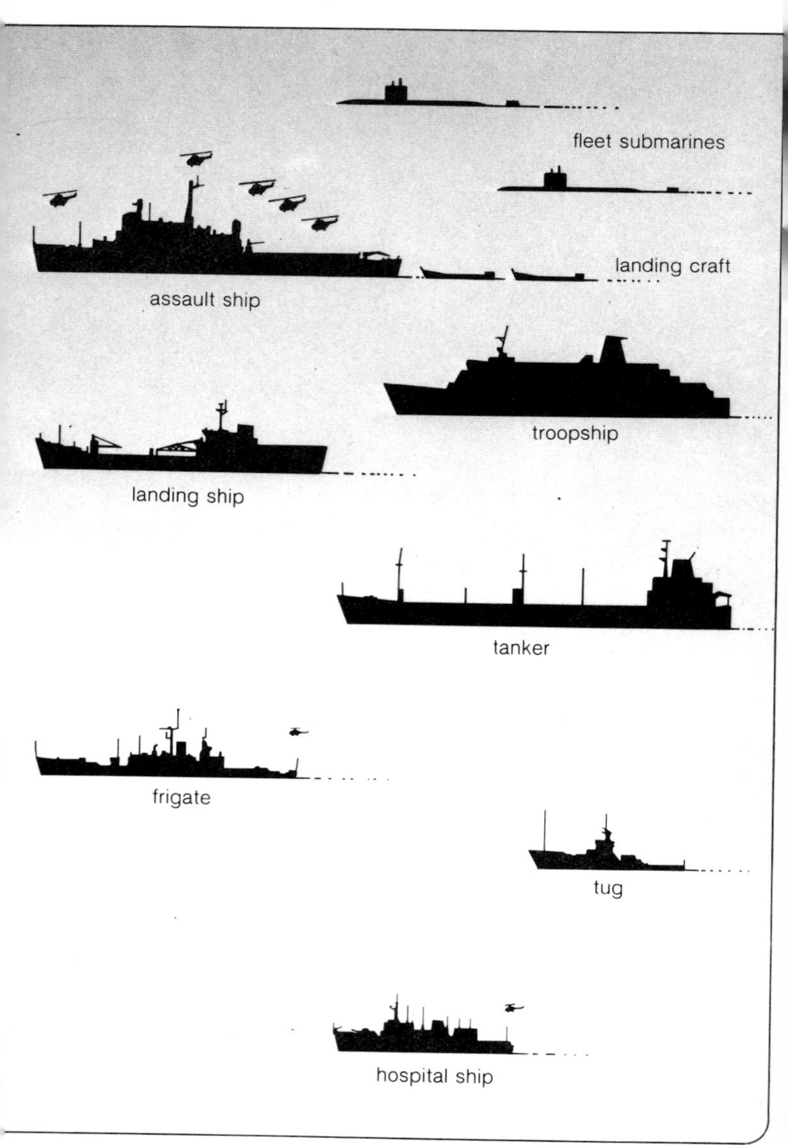
fleet submarines
assault ship
landing craft
troopship
landing ship
tanker
frigate
tug
hospital ship

Index

BEN
OCEAN

BEN OCEAN

SHIPS AND OTHER SEACRAFT

By Brian Williams